EIGHT DOWN

The story of eight maritime disasters over a period of 42 years.

David Reid

Shackleton Partners, LLC

Eight Down

Dedicated to all of the individuals who lost their
lives on the eight ships:
Edmund Fitzgerald
Derbyshire
Marine Electric
Herald of Free Enterprise
Estonia
Sewol
El Faro
Stellar Daisy

In particular the 250 high school students who
perished onboard the *Sewol* in 2014 while on a
school field trip.

Also

In memory of Captain Domenic Calicchio who
campaigned for change within the US Coast Guard.

And

In memory of my sons Mark and Colin – lives brief
in time, significant by their presence.
+++

Eight Down

+++

About the Author

David Reid served in the British Merchant Navy and the Canadian Merchant Marine for eight years at the rank of chief officer. After that, David came ashore to work in the maritime industry of Canada in ship and port operations. David relocated to the United States and has spent the past 40 years as a business leader in ship chartering, stevedoring, port operations, and supply chain management for the steel industry. He is the founder of Shackleton Partners, LLC, a consulting firm serving clients on both sides of the Atlantic for the past 15 years. More recently, David attended seminary and trained to serve as a chaplain, volunteering his time to serve others. David has a master's degree in Interfaith Action.

David joined the Nautical Institute in 1971 and is an Associate Fellow.

He is an ordained minister and serves as a chaplain with the Seamen's Church Institute of Philadelphia and South Jersey.

Preface

42 years, eight maritime disasters, 1509 lives lost. Is there a connective thread?

*E*ight Down reviews eight maritime casualties over 42 years, beginning with the loss of the *Edmund Fitzgerald* on Lake Superior in 1975 to the *Stellar Daisy* in 2017. As a former seafarer and member of the maritime profession for the past 50 years, all of the "Eight" have taken place during my watch. During my research of each incident, I have found a resonance with my own experiences, which has sparked my curiosity. Other authors have written very responsibly about each of these casualties, but each has understandably written with the focus explicit to every single event.

Eight Down will be a review through my personal lens as I explore the connective threads that will illustrate how these events are the consequence of what Professor James Reason has called the "Swiss Cheese Model." I know from my own experience that there were many instances when I might have been but one step away from being a maritime casualty. Is it luck? Or is it the awareness or raised consciousness of someone who acts before that last step occurs? I hope to provide insight into the management of change as it relates to safety, and

Eight Down

how to avoid traveling through the final hole in a "Swiss Cheese."

David Reid MA AFNI
Pequea, PA.
2019

Table of Contents

ONE: MANAGEMENT OF CHANGE   1

TWO: EDMUND FITZGERALD, 1975   15

THREE: DERBYSHIRE, 1980   36

FOUR: MARINE ELECTRIC, 1983   62

FIVE: HERALD OF FREE ENTERPRISE, 1987   76

SIX: ESTONIA, 1994   105

SEVEN: SEWOL, 2014   124

EIGHT: EL FARO, 2015   147

NINE: STELLAR DAISY, 2017   174

TEN: CONNECTING THREADS   213

ELEVEN: LESSONS FROM THE EIGHT   225

BIBLIOGRAPHY   248

ACKNOWLEDGEMENTS   254

GLOSSARY OF TERMS   256

INDEX   261

One: Management of Change

Who and where is the observer? There are times when the observed believes that what they are doing is unseen and that it has not been observed. As a young boy, I made the mistake of riding my bicycle on the wrong side of a road divider on my way home from school. I was observed by a policeman, and a few minutes later he had pulled me over and asked me to explain myself. My feeble excuse was that there was no other traffic around and so I just took the shortcut. He gave me this sage advice, which has remained with me ever since. He said: "There is always someone observing. Even in the middle of the night, somebody will have woken up to look out the window, so never make the mistake of thinking that you are not observed."

Throughout each of the stories that follow in this book, there are situations where people either took action or turned a blind eye in the belief that they were not observed by another. Each step on the pathway towards a disaster is observable, and in many cases, there is no disaster because there is an intervention. However, when the pathway aligns like the "Swiss Cheese Model" described by Professor James Reason, then the disaster has nothing to stop its path, and we are left to observe the sad outcome. The antidote to disaster may be in the hands of the observer. The observer may change the course of events by engaging in dialog with someone about what they have observed. Through each of the eight disasters considered in this book, there are observers who were aware of a latent defect but chose not to say anything. These silent voices are the guardians of latent defects. They provide protection, allowing the holes in the Swiss cheese to align and the event to pass without challenge.

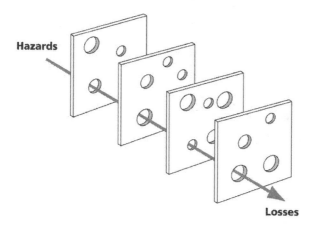

Swiss Cheese Model – by Professor James Reason: CC BY-SA 3.0

Sir Ernest Shackleton is best known for his failed attempt to cross the Antarctic continent in 1914. When their ship the *Endurance* became trapped in the ice, Shackleton wisely transferred the crew and their stores to camp on the ice. In November of 1915, the *Endurance* sank after being crushed by the pressure of the ice pack. The loss of their ship was a severe blow to Shackleton and his 27 crew members. However, Shackleton became famous for the leadership that he gave to the rescue of his entire crew. That rescue involved significant risk, managed entirely by the strength of character delivered by Shackleton against great adversity. Shackleton said that, "Optimism is true moral courage" and "Difficulties are just things to overcome, after all." These sayings, and the actions demonstrated by Shackleton, suggest to me that when he spoke of optimism, he was referring to a greater awareness or a raised consciousness, and it was that state of mind that led to finding true moral courage. During the time after the loss of the *Endurance*, Shackleton was a master of understanding the condition of his 27 men. He did this in a holistic way and considered each of their elements, Mind, Body, and Spirit.

I am confident that Shackleton knew how close they were to failure and never being found. This was long before Professor James Reason gave us the "Swiss Cheese Model." Shackleton had an intuitive awareness that enabled him to navigate his way such that he and his men would not fall prey to passage through the final hole in the "Swiss cheese." Shackleton achieved this through the dynamic management of change, from the time that the *Endurance* became trapped in the ice to the climb across the South Georgia Mountains and glaciers. At each stage, Shackleton embraced the changing circumstances and adapted the plans as the environment around him changed. His only prescription was that of making sure that his crew returned home safely. This required Shackleton to think and act in ways that are today recognized as the tools of leadership. Shackleton made sure that he had the best crew that he could find, and he listened to them. He also understood that some had emotional traits that complicated their technical skills. He made sure that when he left the 22 men on Elephant Island, there was no person amongst them that would create difficulties; instead, Shackleton kept those individuals close by. In many ways, Shackleton was the chaplain to his men. Shackleton provides us with a template for understanding the role of leadership in a maritime setting. He was by profession a merchant mariner who became an explorer. Shackleton had also experienced other leadership styles, most notably while serving as the third officer onboard Sir Robert Falcon Scott's vessel the *Discovery*. Shackleton almost died during Scott's first expedition, and Shackleton witnessed Scott's Royal Navy style of leadership, which was the basic leadership prescription of command and control. Arguably Scott failed because he could not manage change, whereas Shackleton embraced change, learned from it and succeeded.

When a leader is faced with decisions, he must draw upon every component of his knowledge and experience and filter that down to correct action. In some cases, there is time to mull the process of change, and in other cases, there may be hours or just minutes to decide. The special ingredient here is the difficulty of quantifying issues of awareness and levels of consciousness. Throughout my career in the shipping industry, I have mentored my trainees to think of the industry as a multi-story building, with each floor representing a segment of the industry. Consciousness is achieved when you can look through the levels because they are transparent, and you can obtain an awareness of how all the segments connect with each other. On my first visit to the Lloyd's Insurance Building in London, I noted that the architect Richard Rogers designed the atrium space above the underwriting floor to capture such a feeling of transparency. As a navigator, I learned celestial navigation. To fully grasp the relationships of navigating in spherical geometry, there is a need to think transparently to be able to visualize the mechanics of determining where your ship is located. This is also true in many other aspects of the maritime voyage. When planning a complex stowage plan, there is a need to think transparently. When undertaking repairs, there must be an awareness of what is beyond to avoid a mistake. This attitude of situational awareness and the management of change is in itself a driver in the successful management of any enterprise.

There are some managers and leaders who never fully attain the optimum level of awareness and ability to think transparently. Instead, they learn how to follow the traffic and mimic the actions of others. They are typically risk-averse and slow to react to change. Change often overwhelms them because the management of change is not their strength. They prefer to remain silent and complacent, relying on luck rather than intelligence to survive. In each of the eight casualties, there were leaders both onshore and onboard who were tasked with the responsibility to care for their crew, their cargo, and their ship, just as Shackleton had done. When Shackleton lost the *Endurance*, he then focused on his crew. Their mission to cross Antarctica was over, their new mission was to get everyone home safely. Eight serious casualties, beginning in 1975 with the *Edmund Fitzgerald* and continuing until 2017 with the *Stellar Daisy*, display a sequence of events that led to the demise of many, in some cases the entire crew. All could have been avoided if a voice had been listened to. If transparent thinking had caused individuals to avoid complacent thinking, they would have been a near-miss and not a disaster. How many times have individuals not spoken up, or challenged something they considered wrong, because they felt a lack of empowerment to share a view? How many times had individuals deviated from what they know to be safe because they are biased by the politics of their situation?

When faced with the dynamics of ship navigation, time is a constant driver that plays into every decision. There are schedules to be met, and delays increase voyage costs, so prudent action can be considered too prudent. Throughout each of the eight casualties, time is a common factor that is influencing the ability of leadership both ashore and afloat to think transparently. Obviously, slowing down or altering course because of heavy weather represents increased costs, but so too is the cost of damage and, in the extreme, the total loss of the crew, the cargo, and the ship. A good example from history comes from the era of Samuel Plimsoll, the man who gave seafarers the safety of the load line. In the nineteenth century, the coal ships that supplied the energy needs of London became known as the "Coffin ships," because they capsized due to overloading so regularly. However, there was no statutory loading limit, so shipowners pressed their masters to load more cargo. If the ship was lost, they claimed on their Lloyd's insurance policy, as did the owners of the cargo. No rules had been broken.

We also see the problem of complacency, especially on repetitive trade routes where there is a risk of shortcuts and a cavalier attitude because the procedure is routine. Airline pilots are trained in a different culture. They are taught specific techniques to avoid complacency. No matter how many times they have landed or taken off, they follow a rigid checklist. They do this to make sure that nothing has been overlooked. The antidote for complacency is transparent thinking—by practicing this every part of the voyage is seen in the whole and not in slices. This creates situational awareness and a raised consciousness.

My own story began on November 10, 1968. I left the safety of my family home in Pinner, a quiet suburban town in the area of North-west London described by British Poet Laureate John Betjeman as "Metro-land." My decision to join the British Merchant Navy had been a surprise to my family given that there was no known connection with anything maritime on either side of my parent's family. I had been studying mechanical engineering at Southgate Technical college in North London for a year, and I planned to move on to university to study civil engineering, with aspirations of making a career building things. The only connection to anything maritime was my school friend Keith, who had left school to attend the Warsash Maritime school near Southampton. Keith was training to be a marine engineer. However, he had yet to go to sea by the time that I made the decision to embark on an apprenticeship in the Merchant Navy. Looking back on why I chose that path, I remember that I felt called to adventure and I saw the Merchant Navy as a way to gain life experience for a few years and then return to resume my engineering studies—a sort of sabbatical, although I would never have considered that term at the age of 18.

At the British Shipping Federation office in London, they asked me if I wanted to be a Deck, Engineering or Radio cadet? The logical choice would have been to choose engineering, since that had been my recent course of study. I realize now that so much of my life has since hinged on the decision that I made that day. In the space of those seconds, as I pondered my response, I answered, "Deck cadet." It is fortunate that I did not choose Radio, because the role of the Radio officer would disappear a few years later with the introduction of satellites and the demise of Morse code telegraphy. At the Shipping Federation, once I had made the critical choice, the man told me that I was fortunate because he had a good friend who was the personnel officer at a London based shipowner's office, and he would arrange an interview. He assured me that I would be contacted by mail in a few days.

Back home in Pinner, I waited, and a few days later the promised letter arrived. I was requested to attend an interview at 8 Balfour Place in Mayfair with Captain Clipsham, the Marine Superintendent at London and Overseas Freighters. As I walked through Mayfair on that October morning in 1968, I was excited about what lay in front of me. I really had no concept of what I would be doing or where I would be going. However, this was not a prime concern. I was confident that I was making the right decision. The offices were in a typical Mayfair residence that had been converted into offices. The entrance was through white pillars that opened into a grand foyer with a uniformed doorman in attendance. I was ushered into the room to the right, which was a large meeting room with a polished mahogany table and a large ornate chandelier hanging above. The effect was one of splendor and grandeur. A few minutes later Captain Clipsham entered the room and introduced himself. He spoke of the company history and their fleet of ships, but this information washed over me. I was numbed by the surroundings and unable to take in the full extent of what he was saying. The two things I do remember were the articles of agreement that he laid on the table, showing me where I needed to sign and my father to countersign; and the list of the uniform items I needed to acquire before reporting to my first ship. I left not knowing what I would be paid or when I would go and where that might be. I had never thought to ask those questions. The next day my father and I signed the agreement, and I posted it back to the Mayfair office. My father gave me a loan of one hundred pounds based on my agreement to repay five pounds per month from my wages. My mother and I made a trip to London to shop for my uniform at the Merchant Navy uniform shop on Dock Street. We left with a full set of kit that included dress blues, tropical whites, and working khakis. Three weeks passed before I learned more. Two things happened. First, I received my first paycheck of 20 pounds for the month of October, and second, a letter arrived with details of my first ship, the *London Prestige*. Inside the letter was an airline ticket for a flight on November 10, from London to New York and on to Houston. I would be the first person in my family to board a commercial flight. The *London Prestige* was the beginning of my time as a seafarer. I signed on ship's articles on November 15, 1968.

This book is the story of eight notable maritime disasters that have taken place during the 50 years since I chose to become a seafarer. They are not the only tragic events that caused the loss of life at sea during this period. Each one is a story by itself, and for the most part, when investigations and panels of inquiry are held, they rightly focus on the circumstances of each event. Over the years, as each one took place, I read the reports and pondered what led to the loss. I have chosen the eight because each one resonated with me in some way.

My consciousness awoke to this in 2017, after I met a group of Korean-Americans in Philadelphia who wanted to remember the 304 people that were lost onboard the ferry *Sewol* that sank off Jindo Island on April 16, 2014. As one of the volunteer chaplains at the seafarer mission in the port city of Philadelphia, I organized a memorial service that was held in the seafarer chapel. The grief that these people felt about the loss was exacerbated by the fact that they had been let down by their country in terms of the response by the Korean coastguard and the government. A total of 250 of the casualties were high school students on a field trip. They perished because they obeyed the instructions that they had been given to remain in their cabins. I researched the available facts about the *Sewol*, and through my lens, as a professional mariner, I recognized the lapses that led to the Swiss Cheese Model in this instance.

For more than a year, I reflected back to my reading of the events that led to the campaign by the families of the crew to open the inquiry and to reveal the truth about the loss of the *Derbyshire*, a large ore-oil carrier off Japan. In Philadelphia, I met Robert Frump, the author of the book about the loss of the *Marine Electric* off the US East Coast. His book, *Until the Sea Shall Free Them*, shone a light on the failure of the United States Coastguard to enforce regulations. In 2015, the *El Faro* sank with the loss of all hands, and the subsequent inquiry replayed the same narrative that had been discerned in February 1983 when the *Marine Electric* went down.

In 1975, the year that the *Edmund Fitzgerald* went down in Lake Superior, I was sailing as chief officer with a Canadian shipping company that had a strong presence in the Great Lakes. As a deep-sea mariner, I observed how fragile the Laker's were compared to ships built for the ocean. I also had experienced the weather on Lake Superior. I recognized that it exhibited conditions similar to what can be found in the open seas. In 1994, when the Baltic ferry *Estonia* went down, a Russian surveyor shared with me that it was well known that her bow doors had been a problem and he immediately said that he was sure that this had been the cause. I have included the *Herald of Free Enterprise* capsize that took place in 1987 in Zeebrugge harbor because it highlights the issue of systemic failure and the risk of flooding that is at the very heart of every ship that goes down. In the case of the four ro-ro's—the *Herald of Free Enterprise*, *Estonia*, *Sewol* and *El Faro*—there is a strong presence of complacent attitude that develops when the ship is on a regular run, and to some extent, this is also true for the

Edmund Fitzgerald and the *Marine Electric*. Indeed, complacency is a risk that involved them all. It is the moment that something is overlooked or bypassed for the sake of convenience. In each of the losses, there were multiple incidences where the management of change failed and moved them through another hole in their journey through the "Swiss Cheese." During my years at sea, I know now that there were times when my life also passed through holes in the Swiss Cheese Model. Fortunately, I have been blessed to never find that final hole. However, I know that several times I was very close to real danger, and the incidence of a near-miss is well known in safety circles as a way of measuring the actual reality of safety. These are the Eight Down, and I believe that there are connective threads between each of the eight spanning a 42-year time period from 1975 to 2017.

The following chapters will explore the story of each one of the eight. I will illustrate where there may be a common connection that reveals an understanding of what really happened, and in so doing shine some light on how we might prevent future losses. This is the best way to remember all those that lost their lives, making sure that we honor them by learning and adopting an honest awareness and the ability to practice transparent thinking

Two: Edmund Fitzgerald, 1975

My first experience sailing on the Great Lakes came on a ship termed a "Saltie" by those that sail the Great Lakes regularly. The American and Canadian fleets that call the Great Lakes home are predominantly sailing in freshwater, and only the Canadian ships venture down the St Lawrence River into the Gulf of St Lawrence experiencing brackish water. So, when a deep-sea ship enters the locks at St Lambert at the Port of Montreal, they are given the nickname of "Saltie" to designate the fact that these deep-sea tourists are entering into a very different maritime environment. For a Saltie to navigate the 12 hundred miles from Montreal to the head of Lake Superior requires passage across four of the five Great Lakes and using 16 locks that lift the ships vertically by six hundred feet above sea level. The American and Canadian "Lakers" are designed to navigate the locks and river systems efficiently. Deep-sea ships are hybrids that are primarily intended for the open oceans, and that means they are a technical compromise when ordered into the Great Lakes system.

In the summer of 1971, I was senior navigating cadet onboard the British flag vessel *London*

Citizen. After completing a voyage to South Africa, we received orders to proceed to the Mozambique port known then as Lourenco Marques, now known as Maputo. There we would load a full cargo of steel "I" Beams for Detroit and Chicago. We were ill-suited to load a cargo of forty-foot long steel beams; our ship was a traditional tween-decker, and it took over three weeks to fill every space with the long bundles of steel beams. The challenge was that although steel is typically heavy and therefore good bottom weight, the steel beams occupied significant space and there was much void space where beams simply could not fit. As we completed the loading, it became clear that by the time we arrived in Montreal, we would have a critical stability problem. The maximum draft to enter the locks at Montreal is 26 feet, while at sea we could carry extra ballast in the double bottoms to maintain positive stability. However, to pass the 26-foot limit we had to pump out the ballast. We would also have less bunker fuel in our double bottom tanks. As we entered the locks at St Lambert, Montreal, opposite the site of the 1967 World Expo, the stability of our ship was extremely "tender," which means there is a minimal righting force to hold the ship upright and stable. As we made the transit through the lower St Lawrence to Lake Ontario, the pilot remarked on the ship's tender behavior as each helm order was given. When we entered the Welland Canal locks, the condition became worse because we were consuming fuel from our lower tanks. Our ship heeled as we were being raised in the lock, causing the port side of the midships accommodation to graze the lock wall as the *London Citizen* rested like a drunken sailor on the wall. We made it out of the final lock and immediately ballast was taken on to regain stability. This was a clear example of a latent defect. Transverse stability is vital to every merchant ship, and the lack of it can lead to casualty, as it did with the *Sewol* (discussed in Chapter Seven).

We left the port of Chicago with a cargo of wheat bound for Spain, and by the time we departed the Great Lakes, we were all glad to be away and back in saltwater. The experience for a "Saltie" was much hard work and long hours on standby through the many locks. In March 1974, I joined my first Canadian ship, having emigrated to Canada. I had been fortunate to land a position as a navigating officer with one of the large Canadian steamship companies. Over the next two years before the loss of the *Edmund Fitzgerald*, I learned the Great Lakes system and sailed on both conventional straight-deck Lakers and Self-Unloaders. As a trained deep-sea navigating officer, I noticed the variations between the design of the Lakers and the Salties. Most noticeably, the navigating bridge was not in the center—the Lakers were built with the navigating bridge on the bow. This would be unthinkable on a deep-sea ship—who would want to be with their nose in the weather and against the full force of the waves? Shipowners on the Lakes realized they wanted the full expanse of the cargo section of the ship, the working part uninterrupted. The bow section was, therefore, a great place to site the navigating bridge.

Lakers primarily plied in fresh water, so they were not exposed to the corrosive nature of salt water. This meant that ships on the Great Lakes did not succumb to rust and thus their lifespan was at least twice that of a comparable Saltie. One of the Lakers I sailed on was originally a World War II "T2" tanker design built in 1943. She was purchased in 1960 and converted to a straight-deck bulk carrier for service on the Great Lakes, keeping her electric propulsion driven by steam turbine generators. She entered service in 1961 as the *Hilda Marjanne*. I served as the second officer on the *Hilda Marjanne* in the summer of 1974, and that was my first experience onboard a straight-deck Laker. The *Hilda Marjanne* was converted again and renamed the *Canadian Ranger* until being scrapped in 2011, giving in total 68 years of service in one form or another. The *Hilda Marjanne* was one of the vessels engaged in the search and rescue after the *Edmund Fitzgerald* was lost on November 10, 1975.

I observed that Lake Superior differed in important ways from the other four. It was longer and deeper, and to me, as a deep-sea navigator, it looked for all intents and purposes like a deep-sea body of water. It is the second largest freshwater lake in the world. The storms in the late part of the season created waves well beyond those of a tranquil lake. On a deep-sea ship, we had ample freeboard when sailing in the Great Lakes because we were sailing light due to the 26-foot draft limitation. However, Lakers were designed for the 26-foot draft, so their freeboard was much less, and given their 730-foot length that meant the extended cargo deck was exposed to the more massive waves found on Lake Superior. I remember looking aft from the bridge of the *Hilda Marjanne* and watching waves break across the deck. The pencil-like hull of the narrow ship flexed as the shell was twisted by the energy of the swells created by the strong winds. Lakers are designed for efficient loading and unloading; they have a system of hatch covers far different from the hatch covers onboard a deep-sea ship. I had been used to MacGregor style covers—large fabricated steel sections hinged together that were rolled across the hatch opening and then lowered using hydraulics so that their weight compressed a rubber gasket that made them watertight. They were then battened down with cleats and wedges so that once secured they were one and the same with the hull.

Robust hatch covers are critical to seafarers, and when they fail disaster follows, as it did with the *Derbyshire* (Chapter Three) and the *Marine Electric* (Chapter Four). On a Laker, there are two fundamental differences. First, there is a much lower coaming around the hatch opening. This is the vertical height of the steel edge that surrounds the hatch opening and supports the cover. On a Laker, this is typically less than two feet, whereas on a Saltie it is four feet or more. This makes a difference in terms of strength and resistance to waves. The second difference is that the hatch covers on a Laker are simply a rectangular steel plate with lifting lugs that are picked up by a rail mounted crane that runs up and down the length of the deck. Onboard a Laker they call them "lids" not hatch covers, basically because "lids" is a more accurate structural description. The "lids" rest on the low coaming with a rubber gasket and are held in place by hinged Kestner clamps. In my view, they were merely a lid to keep the rain from getting into the hatch, but they were not designed to withstand any waves breaking over the deck. Raymond Ramsay, the author of *For Whom the Bell Tolls*, writes: "It is not known if any pre-production hydrostatic pressure testing on simulation mockups was ever undertaken, even though there is strong evidence that the hatch covers collapsed when excessive waterhead loading would have induced elastic instability [implosive buckling]. Kestner clamps were never intended to protect against such a catastrophic event."

In November 1975, I was embarking as the chief officer on a trans-Atlantic voyage onboard a newly acquired vessel to the Canadian flag. A British bulk carrier had been purchased and put under the Maple Leaf flag and named the *St Lawrence Prospector*. We were loading a cargo of wheat bound for Oslo in Norway. As we prepared for that voyage, I became concerned that the condition of the MacGregor hatch covers was not what they should be. The system works well when it is in good repair. I noticed the gaskets were hard, and some were missing, and side cleats and wedges were either missing or seized and ineffective. I raised my concerns to the company marine superintendent. They were unhappy with my news, and had they not needed my deep-sea qualifications, they might well have replaced me for someone who was less observant or diligent. However, I was young and believed safety at sea was my prime concern. Before we left the St Lawrence River, the company supplied us with boxes of special tar-based tape to apply across all the joints between the sections of the hatch covers. My crew did their best, but in the cold, damp weather it was difficult to get the tape to adhere, and by our first day at sea, the tape had all blown off.

As I was dealing with my own worries heading Eastbound on a great circle route across the North Atlantic to Norway that November, the American Laker *Edmund Fitzgerald* was Eastbound on Lake Superior with a load of iron ore, making her routine run to the steel plants of the lower Great Lakes. I learned a saying from the Chief Mate of the *Hilda Marjanne*: "Run light, run often." This advice was given to me on the dock in Duluth as we loaded a cargo of wheat. On a deep-sea ship, we were trained to load the maximum cargo to squeeze every inch of the draft, and thus the earning capability of more freight. As I chatted with the Chief Mate of the *Hilda Marjanne*, I cross-checked his calculations and asked him why he did not load another 100 tons to offset the fuel that we would burn before we reached the first locks. His reply was "Run light—run often." He also backed it up by saying that as long as he loaded the same number of bushels that was typical, then everyone was happy. This was the code of conduct, and I learned that speed was important. Delays were to be avoided and making trips in a season was more significant than taking the time to squeeze a few more tons onboard. I had seen this ethic at work on the Lakes on my first Canadian ship, a self-unloader named the *Canadian Century* that shuttled back and forth across Lake Erie, making six voyages weekly. She carried steam coal from Ohio to a generating station in Ontario. The challenge was to move as much coal as

22

possible during the season. No time was wasted during docking and undocking, and we did it all without the aid of harbor tugs or pilots. We began loading within minutes of getting our lines secured, and the same was true on the Canadian side. The hatch covers or "lids" were left stacked, and we just sailed back and forth across the lake not just with hatches open but with coal piled up above the coamings.

When I read the story of the *Edmund Fitzgerald* and her ill-fated voyage on Lake Superior in November 1975, I knew that the *Fitz*, as she was known, did not have to end up taking her crew to the bottom of the lake. I believe they were following the code of practice on the lakes to make as many trips as they could during the 1975 season, and if that meant navigating through extreme weather—they believed they were invincible because it was another routine voyage across a lake. The *Fitz* was carrying iron ore in the form of Taconite pellets, Iron ore is a dense cargo that leaves vast volumes of space open inside the cargo hold. The result is that, if a hold is flooded, there is ample space for water. That causes the ship to become heavier rapidly and to sink deeper into the water. The inquiry into the cause of the *Fitz* sinking suggests she was taking on water across the deck and that the "lids" failed and allowed lake water ingress to the cargo holds. This caused her to sink lower with less freeboard, and the situation exacerbated: the deeper she went, the easier it was for the lake water to enter. Eventually, she was overwhelmed and went down. Captain McSorley could have delayed his departure or sought shelter and waited for the storm to pass, but he did not. He did not realize he and his crew had already passed through many holes in their Swiss cheese and his decision to push on would take them all through the final hole. In Chapter Eight we will learn about Captain Davidson and the *El Faro*, another case of latent defects being activated by lack of dialog allowing a catastrophe to take the ship and all her crew through that final hole.

In his book *Mighty Fitz*, Michael Schumacher wrote about the testimony given at the inquiry. "Other witnesses maintained that it wasn't at all uncommon for crews to fasten down only half of the hatch cover clamps, especially during the summer months, when the weather was good, and there was no danger of encountering heavy seas. Witnesses also testified that a ship would sometimes leave the dock before the clamps had been dogged down, or that clamps might be removed before it arrived for loading." The testimony of a former First Mate Andrew Rajner described Captain McSorley directing him to fasten down only every other clamp. As Schumacher wrote, "The implication of Zabinski's line of questioning was clear: if the *Fitzgerald* had left Superior on November 9 with only some hatch covers secured, it might have been impossible to fasten them later, when the weather had deteriorated and going out on the deck was dangerous." (Captain Zabinski was one of the four members of the Coast Guard Marine Board of Investigation.)

I came across a video posted on the Internet by students from Aristoi Academy in Texas who compiled a report on the *Edmund Fitzgerald*. It can be found at the following link: https://www.aristoiclassical.org/apps/video/watch.js p?v=88217

The footage shows what appears to be the *Edmund Fitzgerald* in heavy weather. The funnel markings are the same. What is noticeable is that some hatch covers have only half of the Kestner clamps fitted, and others appear to have none. In the background, a large wave can be seen just starting to break across the aft deck.

Schumacher summarized the findings from the Marine Board inquiry thus: "The most probable cause of the sinking was the loss of buoyancy resulting from massive flooding of the cargo hold. The flooding most likely took place through ineffective hatch closures. As the boarding seas rolled over the spar deck, the flooding was probably concentrated forward. The vessel dove into a wall of water and never recovered, with the breaking up of the ship occurring as it plunged or as the ship struck the bottom. The sinking was so rapid and unexpected that no one was able to successfully abandon ship."

The finding of the Marine Board inquiry resonates with my own experiences on the Great Lakes. I observed first-hand the broad difference of understanding between Lakers and Salties concerning watertight integrity. The former is a different type of seamanship that is a direct result of sailing in enclosed waters and usually not during the winter season. Lake Superior in November brought a taste of what the deep-sea sailor faces daily in the North Atlantic in winter. There is one further point of difference and Schumacher makes a note of this when discussing the information gained from the *Arthur M. Anderson*, the ship shadowing the *Fitzgerald* across Superior that night. Schumacher wrote, "In its reconstruction, the Marine Board focused strongly on the conversations between Captains McSorley and Cooper, particularly the one during which McSorley had informed Cooper that the *Fitzgerald* had lost a fence rail and two vents and had developed a list. To that point, the *Fitz* had been running smoothly, with no report of damage. The loss of the ship's radar, along with the *Fitz's* slowing down to allow the *Anderson* to close the distance between the two ships, was significant, especially since no formal track line charts of the two vessels had been kept." I know from my own experience as a navigator on Canadian Lakers that marking the ship's position or track on the charts was not the standard practice. I was once chastised by a master for marking the ship's position on the chart, being told it was unnecessary. In my training as a deep-sea navigator, this was the exact opposite of what a watch-keeping officer should do. Marking and tracking the ship's position was a routine procedure. As evidenced by the report, the *Arthur M. Anderson* kept no record of her own position nor that of the *Fitz* except for the pencil line that showed the route they had been on.

Complacency and a false sense of security may have been the root cause behind the failure to secure the hatch covers. Schumacher quotes C. S. Loosmore, one of the four members of the Marine Board, who said the following: "They knew they had all those hatch clamps, but they didn't need them." Loosmore rejected the speculation that McSorley might have been trying to save overtime expenses by ordering only some of the clamps fastened down. Loosmore went on, "I think they were complacent. They had done this kind of thing with no damage, no problem at all, for years and years." The task of battening down all of the Kestner clamps was a formidable one for the three deckhands on the *Fitzgerald*. Simple mathematics shows that if just one minute was allocated for each clamp to be positioned and secured, the total time required would be 23.8 man-hours. (Note: one Kestner clamp per minute assumes no adjustment is needed to ensure that the clamp is fully secure, and the reality is it would have taken more than one minute per Kestner clamp.) For the three deckhands, this would take them each at least 8 hours or longer. They departed Superior at 2 pm on November 9. Whether they worked late into that night "dogging" hatch covers is now unknown. Most probable is they only fitted a few on each hatch cover around each corner, which in my experience was the common practice on the Great Lakes.

The NTSB inquiry concurred with the Coast Guard Marine Board concerning the massive flooding of the cargo holds but held that prior flooding into the ballast tanks and tunnel had made a prior contribution to the reduction of freeboard before the failure of the hatch covers.

The deposition provided by Carl Burgner, a former long-serving crew member from the *Fitzgerald*, provided insight into the work ethic that he had experienced during his many years sailing on the *Fitzgerald*. Schumacher wrote, "Burgner's deposition represented by far the most critical statement issued to that point on the events leading to the accident. Burgner testified favorably about McSorley and Mcarthy's (chief mate of the Fitzgerald) knowledge and abilities, but he also made it clear that he felt McSorley was a company man who 'beat hell' out of the Fitzgerald in nasty weather in order to deliver his cargo on schedule. Not only did McSorley rarely anchor his ship and wait out a storm; he rarely slowed down in heavy weather, thus exposing his ship to greater pounding from the seas."

The Coast Guard Marine Board and the NTSB inquiries tell us one part of the story that led to the loss of the 29 onboard the *Edmund Fitzgerald*. There is another part, and that is the root cause of the latent defects and the dialog that allowed the alignment to occur, leading to the demise of the *Fitzgerald*. Consider three aspects: First, the work ethic that Burgner described of driving hard to maintain the schedule of trips each season. McSorley was not alone, he was likely part of a culture condoned and encouraged within the company. Where were the challenges from his superiors to reinforce productivity with safety? Sadly, this is the missing ingredient in the dialog, and an unwritten code of machoism can develop that causes masters like McSorley to push harder. I witnessed this culture at work on the Great Lakes, and sadly Captain McSorley was more than likely a victim of an embedded ethic not of his own design.

Second, the hatch covers fitted to Lakers were not designed by McSorley or any of his crew, they were the creation of a naval architect charged with finding a compromise between production efficiency and safety. The design had to be a low-cost component of the ship's building price and simple to operate in terms of removal and placement of covers. The traveling deck crane mounted on rails enabled one crewman to lift and carry the "lids" and stack them clear for cargo operations. However, for watertight securing the "lids" were labor intensive, firstly because there were so many "lids" to secure (21 in all) and there are 68 Kestner clamps around the perimeter of each "lid." Lastly, unless the clamps and the watertight gasket are properly maintained, there can be no watertight integrity against seas on deck.

In designing this type of hatch cover system, the shipowner and the shipbuilder had a dialog about what I can best describe as the "hatch cover of convenience." By this, I mean they were convenient to everyone except those that had the task of battening them down and depending on them for their safety. As a chief mate on a Canadian Laker, I sailed with this system of hatch covers, and I pushed my deck crew to make sure that every clamp was secured and screwed tight. I paid particular attention because my ship navigated both the Great Lakes and the East Coast. However, I was trained as a deep-sea mate, and that caused me to act in a different way to my Lakes counterparts. Third, complacency is the virus that invades the workplace and causes paralysis of dialog, the inability to challenge, the reluctance to step forward. This is a malaise that is particularly prevalent when ships are engaged on repetitive voyages. During my time at sea, I observed the difference in culture between the life of a tramp steamer that meanders around the world taking on new courses and ports as a routine, and the shuttle run where familiarity can lead to inattentiveness. When you are challenged to tackle unfamiliar places, there is a need to be mindful and a basis for dialog to ask the right questions. Conversely, such dialog can be suppressed and missing when complacency is allowed into the environment. This syndrome appears in Chapter Four with the *Marine Electric* and again in Chapter Five with the *Herald of Free Enterprise*.

The findings from the Marine Board of Inquiry said the following with respect to the hatch closings:

> Recommendation 3.
> "That the owners and operators of Great Lakes ore carrying vessels undertake a positive and continuing program of repair and maintenance to insure [*sic*] that all closures for openings above the freeboard deck are weathertight, that is, capable of

preventing the penetration of water into the ship in any sea condition. This program should include frequent adjustment of hatch clamping devices and vent closures and prompt repair of all hatches, coamings, covers, and clamping devices found damage or deteriorated."

Recommendation 5.
"That the Coast Guard undertake a program to evaluate hatch closures presently used on Great Lakes ore carriers with a view toward requiring a more effective means of closure of such deck fittings."

The Coast Guard commandant added the following Action.

"1.b. Bring to the attention of the owners and operators the fact that weathertight closures which are not effective when battened down void both the LOAD LINE CERTIFICATE and the CERTIFICATE OF INSPECTION."

Notably, in the NTSB report they included the following statement, including the results of Coast Guard inspections that had taken place after the loss of the *Edmund Fitzgerald*:

"Each clamp had an adjustment bolt which determined the force applied by the individual clamp and therefore controlled the deflection of the hatch cover, the compression of the rubber gasket, and the weathertightness of the hatch opening. There were no written procedures concerning maintenance or adjustment of the hatch clamps or gaskets."

"Visual inspections by Coast Guard Marine Inspections during the winter of 1976 and the spring of 1977 and by Safety Board personnel during the summer of 1977 indicate that hatch covers on Great Lakes vessels are not maintained weathertight."

Latent defects are all around us, and from a medical perspective they are also within us. They are, as Professor Reason explains, the pathogens that await a trigger. In the case of the *Edmund Fitzgerald*, the findings of the inquiries suggest the latent defects existed, and they were merely waiting for the moment when the alignment would occur. The pathogens could have remained dormant had a different dialog taken place. Suppose for a moment that the culture had been different between the owners of the *Fitzgerald* and Captain McSorley. Might they have had a dialog about the weather forecast before the departure from Superior and made a decision to delay sailing to let the weather system pass? Suppose that Captain McSorley had engaged in a dialog with his chief mate McCarthy prior to the end of the 1975 Lakes season about the maintenance and integrity of the hatch covers. Could such a dialog have reinforced a stronger importance to making sure that all the Kestner clamps were fitted correctly and secured prior to those November voyages? Suppose that onboard the *Fitzgerald* the leadership had engaged in a dialog to ward off the ills of complacency. Such action would have been noticed by crew members like Burgner.

The reality of the *Edmund Fitzgerald* and her crew remain a secret. As always, there are those who seek truth to apportion blame, and there are others who seek to understand. The challenge of every person charged with the responsibility of investigation is how to navigate through the available evidence to create the reconstruction. This is no simple task, and it is made harder when other agendas seek to divert attention or create a distraction to shield a party from liability. The holistic view of the *Edmund Fitzgerald*, therefore, requires an understanding of the dialog that created the operating culture and how that played its part in setting up the opportunity for the latent defects to seize control of the *Fitzgerald*. The men of the *Fitzgerald* fell to their deaths in November 1975 not because the *Fitzgerald* was unique: many, if not all, ships have the potential to receive the same fate. The difference is the interaction of individuals who choose to intervene. In *For Whom the Bell Tolls*, Raymond Ramsay summarizes this succinctly as the following: "As a retired third-generation shipbuilder, I firmly believe that a lifelong social contract should prevail between shipowners, designers, shipbuilders, and operating crews." Ramsay's social contract is the dialog essential to preventing the lethal pathogens (latent defects) from being released.

Three: Derbyshire, 1980

September 10 happens to be my birthday. That was the day in 1980 when the *Derbyshire* was lost. At that time, I was living in Saint John, New Brunswick, Canada. I had stopped going to sea in the latter part of 1976. I had served over two years on Canadian owned ships. I was fortunate to come ashore to work as the marine superintendent for the Canadian steamship company that I had sailed for as chief officer. In the fall of 1977, I had been hired by a stevedoring company to serve as their operations manager in the Port of Saint John. During my time at sea, I had frequently loaded iron ore at the Quebec ports of Sept Iles, Pointe Noire, and Havre St Pierre. On that day, I was celebrating my thirtieth birthday. The British ore/bulk/oil carrier *Derbyshire* was battling her way through Typhoon Orchid to Kawasaki, Japan, with her full cargo of 157,000 tons of Canadian iron ore concentrate that had been loaded at the port of Sept Iles, Quebec. Sadly, the *Derbyshire* went down on that day, taking her entire crew and two officer's wives to their death.

The story of the *Derbyshire* resonates on many levels. The ship had been built by Swan Hunter on Teesside in 1976, a place that I would call home 30 years later while I worked as the supply chain director at the Redcar Steelworks. The Redcar Steelworks was one of the major industries present on the Tees, during the building of the "Bridge" class OBO's (ore-bulk-oil carrier) at the Haverton Hill shipyard. The Teesside and Scunthorpe mills owned by British Steel were the principal source of the steel used to construct the Bridge-class OBO's. British Steel and the successor owner Corus embraced using cape-size bulk carriers to carry their iron ore and coal feedstock. The Redcar works alone required 5 million tons of iron ore and 2.5 million tons of coking coal to maintain its 3 million tons of raw steel output. By the 1980s all the UK steelworks had either direct port facilities or nearby third-party capability to facilitate reception of cape-size shipments. Redcar had its own deepwater bulk terminal capable of handling large cape-size bulk carriers and discharging up to 50,000 tons per day. Redcar had the capability of feeding directly from the ship to the blast furnace by belt conveyor, although this was rarely needed since a sizable inventory was always available in the yard.

Ore carriers experience tremendous stress both during loading and unloading. Iron ore is dense and gets loaded at speed off the end of a fast conveyor belt and into the ship's hold. To avoid excessive bending moments and shear stress, the loading rotates among different holds to load the ship evenly on a longitudinal basis. In a standard bulk carrier designed for various bulk cargoes, the cargo holds are designed to offer a maximum cubic capacity so that high-density cargo can be fully accommodated. However, iron ore has a low density and therefore if all cargo holds are loaded, the center of gravity of the cargo is low, and this results in a large metacentric height or "GM." The result is that the ship has a short rolling period and is considered "stiff." This stability condition results in violent rolling acceleration on the higher decks of the ship. To offset this and to afford simpler loading with fewer moves, faster unloading with more free-digging for the grabs and less machine time in the cargo holds, the concept of alternate hold loading was permitted. This left some holds empty with greater longitudinal shear stress at the bulkheads. However, the GM was reduced, resulting in a more comfortable rolling action. For shippers and receivers, the loading and discharge was more efficient. In particular, at discharge, the ore is removed by heavy grabs and the longer the free-digging time, the faster the discharge. Fewer holds with cargo equate to less time needed for bulldozers and wheeled loaders inside the hold to bring the ore under the reach of the grab. The plating on the floor of the cargo holds known as the tank-top becomes dimpled as the plating is stretched between the supporting girders below. In a typical bulk carrier, the entire structure below the tank-top is visible as if on an x-ray. Grab damage to the tank-top plating and to the side tanks is not unusual and must be repaired before sailing—assuming that is has been noticed.

Purpose built ore carriers have a different design because they do not need the high cubic capacity that is required for grain or coal. I sailed as chief mate onboard one such purpose designed ore carrier built by the American Industrialist Daniel Ludwig. The *Ore Transport* was built in 1954 at the Kure shipyard in Japan. With a deadweight of 59,580 tons, the *Ore Transport* was one of the largest ore carriers in the world.

She was a twin boiler ship with twin turbines driving twin screws. Her cargo holds were box-shaped with no wings. The double bottoms under the cargo holds were 20 feet in depth. This kept the cargo at a higher center of gravity and the GM in the comfort zone. After 20 years under National Bulk Carriers, the ship was sold to Canadian owners and renamed the *Canadian Transport*. I sailed on the ship when she was 22 years old, and she remained extremely robust with not a ripple in her hull plating. This class of innovative ships were built with a heavier structure far in excess of anything that I experienced on any other ship. This was evident in her lightship displacement. From memory it was circa 20,000 tons, and this was almost three times the mass of a modern Panamax bulk carrier that I had sailed on. The enhanced scantlings were evident on the hull plating, the framing, and girders inside the large side tanks. The two steam windlasses on the forecastle had immense power. We frequently anchored loaded with 45,000 tons of ore in the St Lawrence River off the port of Sorel. We put down two anchors due to the current. Amazingly, we could engage both windlasses and heave up both cables against the current with no main engine power. This is a feat that exemplifies the high standard of marine engineering that went into the design of the Ludwig ships.

In the 1950s Daniel Ludwig pioneered the innovation of the ore carrier at the Kure shipyard, building a series of ships that would shuttle iron ore from the Orinoco River in Venezuela to feed the demand at US Steel's East Coast steelworks. During the same era on the other side of the Atlantic, British Steel languished, with port facilities unable to accommodate larger ships. So, British Steel turned to a cadre of British shipowners and chartered a fleet of small ore carriers that became known as the BISCO Ore Carrier Fleet. Familiar British shipowners including Buries Markes, Common Bros, Corys, Denholms, Dalgleish, Houlders, Lyle, Ropner, Silver Line, Souter, and

Welsh Ore Carriers were all part of this vast iron ore navy. However, this fleet would be made redundant with the advent of new larger port facilities and a new breed of cape-size ships.

The Lord Donaldson report from the initial inquiry in 1998 placed the blame on an unsecured stores hatch cover on the foredeck, which were attributed to crew error. The Final Inquiry by Justice Colman in 2000 revealed that the fault lay with ventilation pipes that failed under the impact of heavy seas, allowing sea water ingress, which was not the fault of the crew. This caused the bow of the ship to sink, and the number one hold hatch cover collapsed under the weight of green seas. The continued entry of seawater caused the *Derbyshire* to capsize very fast bow down. The design of the *Derbyshire* did not consider the risk of failure in the ventilation pipes located on the exposed foredeck. Unlike other ship designs, the *Derbyshire* did not have a raised bow with a forecastle. The foredeck was simply a continuation of the main deck.

The design of the *Derbyshire* as a hybrid was designed to be both a bulk carrier and a tanker. The design required the ability to have the pipework and pumping systems of a tanker while having hatch covers for handling bulk cargo. Shipowners when planning to order a new ship may have the luxury of ordering on a firm contract they hold, or they may be speculating about the forward market and trying to build a ship that will be launched into a market where that type is in short supply. In such a case, they can charter at a premium and earn back their cost of capital. The lead time for ordering, building, and delivery requires a shipowner building in speculation to have a crystal ball because several years can elapse. Over the years when the tanker market had collapsed some shipowners sought to convert their tankers to dry bulk carriers rather than remain in lay-up. This was the case on my first ship the *London Prestige* that began its life as a tanker and then became a bulk carrier. In chapter four we will discuss the *Marine Electric* which also was launched as a T2 tanker to be converted to a bulk carrier, and in chapter eight we will look at the *El Faro* which was converted from a Ro-Ro to a Ro-Ro/Container vessel.

To unpack the loss of the *Derbyshire*, we have to take a holistic view of both the design and the operation. At Swan Hunter in Teesside when the *Derbyshire* was built, her first name was the *Liverpool Bridge*, and she was one of a series of six that had the same design. Entering service in 1976, she was only four years old at the time of the loss; however, two of those years had been in lay-up when the shipping market had slumped to bleak demand even for a hybrid design. The inquiry revealed that Captain Underhill had taken precautions and hove to while battling Typhoon Orchid. However, he would not have been aware of the flooding taking place in the forward compartments and the increased forward draft. The technology to remotely sensor bilges was not a requirement for the *Derbyshire*, and the conventional system of taking soundings manually could not take place during heavy weather. No crew member could venture forward on the exposed deck to take manual soundings. In the case of the *Derbyshire*, the Swiss cheese path suggests the naval architects failed to recognize the vulnerability of the ventilation pipes on the exposed foredeck. The increased submersion of the bow then led to the forward cargo hatches being exposed to more heavy seas crashing down and overwhelming their capacity to withstand the immense weight of water.

The lack of a forecastle resulted in the main deck being more exposed and afforded no protection to ventilation pipes which can be sited in the lee of the forecastle where one is provided. The lack of a forecastle appears consistent with tanker hulls, while bulk carriers typically are designed with a forecastle. The salient difference is that bulk carriers have large hatch covers on deck and a raised forecastle serves to protect the main deck. Tankers have pipework, manholes, and vents, but the decks are otherwise clear and offer minimal obstruction to seas washing over the deck.

The *Derbyshire* was not the only bulk carrier without a forecastle to be lost without a distress signal and with all hands. In 1990 and 1991 there were four ships without forecastles lost with no survivors. Two of them were OBO's like the *Derbyshire*.

In March 1990, the 95k deadweight bulk carrier *Alexandre P* was lost in the South Indian Ocean en route from Dampier in Western Australia to Gijon in Spain via the Cape of Good Hope.

In April 1991, the 142k deadweight bulk carrier *Mineral Diamond was* lost during Cyclone Fifi in the South Indian Ocean while en route with iron ore from Dampier in Western Australia to Ijmuiden in the Netherlands via the Cape of Good Hope.

In August 1990, the 155k deadweight Ore-Bulk-Oil carrier *Pasithea* was lost off the Japanese port of Kashima during Typhoon Vernon carrying a cargo of iron ore. There is a YouTube video of the *Pasithea* at sea while on a loaded voyage that illustrates the open exposure of her foredeck without the benefit of a forecastle. It can be found at https://www.youtube.com/watch?v=8eCdg91RuRU

In September 1990, the 135k deadweight OBO *Algarrobo* was lost in the South Pacific Ocean having sailed from Huasco, Chile with a cargo of iron ore destined for Kawasaki, Japan

The phenomenon of ships encountering abnormal waves is not uncommon, and I observed the dramatic impact of what can happen when I saw the British cargo liner the *Bencruachan* at the port of Durban in 1973. The *Bencruachan* was one of the fast cargo liners owned by Ben Line. She was on the last day of her voyage from Singapore to Durban, South Africa when she encountered an abnormal wave in the night. My ship was berthed ahead of the *Bencruachan*. I was Second Officer on the *London Statesman*. I walked along the dock at Durban and stood looking at the bow tilted downwards by about 20 degrees. The hull plating had been folded like the pleats in a kilt, and her forward hatch cover was wrapped around the foremast.

They never realized the extent of the damage until daylight. The *Bencruachan* limped into Durban and was towed stern-first back to Europe for major repairs. Looking at the damage gave me an entirely renewed insight into just how powerful the energy at sea can be. The reality of what happened to the *Bencruachan* is that naval architects are not designing for such events, because they were believed to be a fiction, the rogue or freak wave. Science relied on the linear model of wave analysis,

45

which held that rogue waves could not exist. This all changed after the data provided by the Statoil offshore platform *Draupner* located in the North Sea. Statoil had fitted their offshore platforms with a radar sensor to study and record wave heights. On January 1, 1995, the *Draupner* experienced a wave of 25.9 meters. The platform had been designed to withstand waves of 19.5 meters. The data from the *Draupner* proved the linear model was in error and opened the door to further research on a global scale.

In the case of the *Derbyshire*, the small ventilation pipe on the foredeck was not risk assessed to simulate the impact of how a failure could result in the flooding of the forepeak tank and the consequent effect of a bow down situation with green seas crashing on to the exposed forward hatch covers.

There is a vast difference between a mathematical simulation and the real situation. Under actual conditions, there are multiple forces at play, and when there is a coincidence, the openings in the "Swiss Cheese" align.

Google Earth makes it possible for anyone to view coordinates of latitude and longitude. Using the known position of the *Derbyshire* wreck and the last known positions of other ships, it is possible to see the terrain of the ocean floor in incredible detail. Mariners know well that the behavior of the sea at the surface can be profoundly affected by the terrain below. When storms move over deep water, and then approach shallower depths the stored energy causes strange behavior in the swells. Certain areas of the world are renowned for their unpredictable conditions where strong currents and changing underwater terrain create abnormal sea conditions. The Indian Ocean coast off South Africa and the Bay of Biscay are but two examples. When you view the location of the *Derbyshire* wreck, it is located in deep water but surrounding that location there are underwater ridges that create a resistance to the movement of the ocean waves, and this may have contributed to the conditions for abnormal wave activity.

I experienced abnormal wave activity on two occasions, once in the Pacific and the second time in the Indian Ocean off South Africa. They were some years apart but both on the same ship, the *London Statesman*. We had departed the port of Durban with a cargo of raw sugar, and as we sailed southwest towards the Cape of Good Hope, we had the benefit of the strong Agulhas current pushing us faster, so we were making over 16 knots. However, we had deep swells coming from the southeast, and this was causing us to roll heavily. The winds were light, but the swells were long and deep. I was the second mate, and during my afternoon watch, I was observing the swells and the rolling. I had just seen the damaged *Bencruachan*, and I was mindful of what had happened to her. In the middle of my watch, we were rolling heavily more than 20 degrees, and that sends everything flying as the ship makes a forty-degree sweep from side to side. I stood by the helm, holding on to the steering stand and watched the brass clinometer swing over, indicating the angle of each roll. As I watched, I counted the angle, and each successive roll was a few degrees greater than the last. Within the space of a few minutes, we were nearing a roll of 30 degrees, and I then realized that what I was observing was a phenomenon known as synchronous rolling. I had listened to Graham Danton, our lecturer at Plymouth College, speak about this, and the belief that this phenomenon was responsible for the loss of the British passenger liner *Waratah* off the South African coast on or about July 28, 1909. The *Waratah* had also sailed from Durban headed to Cape Town. I was alone on the bridge, and I had no time to consult with anyone, so I made my decision to take the ship out of auto-pilot and go to manual steering. As we came out of the next heavy roll, I applied ten degrees of starboard helm to change course and to break the rhythm of the rolling period. As the bow moved to starboard, we began our next roll to port but the change of course worked, and that roll was less than before. I kept that course for the next few hours until the chief mate relieved me at 16:00. I believe that on that afternoon in 1973, I experienced a moment when the fate of my life, my shipmates and the *London Statesman* all hung for a few seconds on what my brain would tell me to do. To this day I believe Graham Danton's lecture was the dialog that saved us from the same fate as the *Waratah*. The *Waratah* disappeared without a trace, and 211 passengers and crew were lost. (Graham Danton is the author of *The Theory and Practice of Seamanship*.)

My first trip aboard the *London Statesman* was in 1969, and we were westbound across the Pacific from Portland, Oregon bound for Tokyo. We were down to summer marks and sailing on the edge of the permitted summer zone in the winter storm season. We had a lot of deck cargo consisting of drums of a dangerous chemical called Tetra-ethyl lead, the anti-knock compound used as a fuel supplement in Japanese cars. The drums were heavily secured on both sides of the deck between the bulwarks and the hatch coamings. The 55-gallon drums were all interlocked together and tied down with wire rope lashings. As an extra precaution before leaving Portland, the charterers had arranged for a wooden breakwater to be built on the forward end of the drums on the foredeck. Massive 12 x 12 timbers were wedged across between the hatch coaming and the bulwark, then faced with one-inch sheets of plywood to create a wall. Holes were left in the plywood to allow some water to flow through. I watched these being constructed. They were very robust. In my humble opinion as a cadet, I believed these would do the job.

How wrong I was. During our first day at sea the wooden walls simply disappeared as we plunged into the Pacific waves. Over the next days and weeks, we battled storm after storm. The drums were being battered, and you could see them beginning to move as the lashings failed. Finally, drums broke free, popping out of the group like a cork from a bottle. We hove to, and our Filipino deck crew went out on deck to jettison the loose drums over the side, no easy task when the ship was still pitching and rolling. They struck the drums with a fire ax so the contents could spill out. The rest of the drums were secured as best as could be done, and we resumed our voyage. A few days later on a Sunday evening, we had another emergency when the starboard lifeboat broke free of its lashings in the davits, we all turned to and watched our principal motor lifeboat swinging around on its wire falls—a scary sight when the lifeboat is your principal means of escape. The lifeboat was brought under control, fortunately without damage. As the days went on, there were many days when we literally went nowhere. The swells were so high and deep they lifted the ship up and brought the propeller out of the water. This caused the engine to race as the propeller had no resistance. Being unable to make way, we kept enough power to maintain steering control while being pitched like a cork. This was only my second ship, and so I was new to this. I do remember the dark mood that descended on everyone. There were long faces and little conversation. I do recall looking astern one morning and seeing the stern race downwards in the trough. As we descended, I looked at the towering wall of water that rose above us. It was higher than the beam of our ship. Our beam was 65 feet, and I was looking at a 75-foot wave. At the time, I did not know how significant that was, but in the years that followed I would. By the time we reached Tokyo Bay we were out of heavy fuel oil—our week of delays had caused us to use all our reserve fuel. As we sailed those last miles, the engineers said we were literally running on fumes. We were anchored in a quarantine area and were met by a bunker barge; the Japanese authorities came on board wearing breathing apparatus and protective clothing. They were afraid of the fumes from the Tetra-ethyl lead spill. They took away our clothing for de-contamination and spent days testing before we were allowed into port.

My experiences onboard the *London Statesman* revealed to me the incredible forces that can be encountered at sea. As a mariner, I can understand why linear models of wave theory do not apply to the reality of what mariners have been experiencing and reporting for many years. Francesco Fedele, Professor of Engineering at the Georgia Institute of Technology, specializes in fluid and wave mechanics. Fedele said, "Just accounting for asymmetry can increase the crest height by 20%. Past linear simulations failed because they did not account for irregular wave peaks and other unpredictable factors. Models based on modulation instability also ran aground because the underlying concept applies to circumstances in which a wave travels along a narrow, one-way corridor, as light waves do in an optical fiber. This is not important in the ocean because there are no boundaries."

In February 2000 the British oceanographic research vessel the *Discovery* recorded a 61-foot significant wave height (mean wave height) and individual waves of 95 feet. Radar images from a European Space Agency satellite have found rogue waves of 82 feet or higher. The *Draupner* wave in the North Sea provided the maritime community with the proof that rogue or freak waves are not a fiction, they are real.

A report by Sverre Haver of Statoil, the owner of the *Draupner* platform, cited the following about the wave event January 1, 1995, in a paper presented in 2003.

"A number of people and institutions have been given access to the *Draupner* time history. I think there is a general agreement that the wave event can be referred to as a freak event, i.e., an event that would not be expected under our typical engineering models for extreme wave predictions. I think there are competing ideas regarding explaining the event and not least regarding modeling it mathematically, but my favorite theory involves self-focusing of energy of a wave group into one majestic wave event, i.e., the big event steals energy from its neighbors. The major challenge from my point of view is to understand when and why this strongly non-linear self-focusing process is turned on."

Unfortunately, the data and awareness came long after the loss of the *Derbyshire* and many other ore carriers. However, when Justice Colman chaired the second inquiry from April 5, 2000 to July 26, 2000, this was five years after the *Draupner* incident, more than sufficient time for rogue waves to be considered. Section 37 of the Colman report states:

"These conditions had deteriorated in the
course of 8, and 9, September. The hindcast
evidence is to the effect that for about 12
hours from 0500z on 9, September the route of
the *DERBYSHIRE* experienced significant
wave heights above 9.5 meters (31 feet), rising
to a peak of 10.85 meters (36 feet) by 1700z.
The vessel's average forward speed in these
conditions would be in the range 1.50 to 2
knots over the ground depending on wave drift
forces. That would have taken the vessel to the
wreckage site by about 1700z to 2000z on that
day."

However, as we now know from the research that
has followed after the *Draupner* incident, there is a
possibility that within that significant wave height
of 10 meters (33 feet) there may well have been a
wave of much greater height like the one
experienced by the *Draupner*.

In section 42, the report moves on to discuss the
consequence of the impact of green seas landing on
the No. 1 hatch and draws the conclusion that even
at a wave height of 10.85 meters the condition
would have exceeded the strength of the hatch
covers. We will never know for sure what
happened, but we now know that the existence of
rogue waves is real, and the *Derbyshire* may have

encountered one during the turbulent sea conditions that are typical during a Typhoon.

"The results of those tests indicated that at speeds of zero or 2 knots, without water ingress, at the peak significant wave height of 10.85 meters, and even at 12.5 meters, the maximum loading on No.1 hatch would be well below the collapse strength. However, in the damaged condition, with the bow flooded, the maximum measured impacts on No.1 hatch at a significant wave height of 10.85 meters exceeded its collapse strength, even at zero speed."

The loss of the *Derbyshire* led to a twenty-year campaign by the Derbyshire Families Association, who tirelessly devoted their lives to finding the truth. The first inquiry by Wreck Commissioner Gerald Darling was held from October 1987 to March 1988 and reached its findings without the benefit of the underwater survey that took place in 1997 and 1998. Darling found the *Derbyshire* was overwhelmed by the forces of nature. In 1994 the ITF agreed to fund an underwater search to locate the wreck, and they succeeded even though it was in very deep water (4200 meters). The UK Department of Transport then appointed Lord Donaldson to advise of the benefit of an underwater survey. The Donaldson Report held the main reason for the flooding of the bosun's stores to be the failure of the crew to secure the store's hatch properly. This implied there had been failure or negligence on the part of the crew, and the Derbyshire Families Association were upset. Following the Donaldson report, then Deputy Prime Minister John Prescott announced the formal investigation was to be re-opened at the High Court under Justice Colman.

Justice Colman's report focused on the role of Ocean-routes, and this was cited in section 27 as follows: "The vessel was also receiving occasional weather reports from Ocean-routes, a routing agency appointed by the charterers." In section 28 the report stated, "At no time did Ocean-routes advise the master to alter course to avoid the typhoon." In section 35 the report added, "However, the brochure issued to masters by Ocean-routes in which it set out what routing services it would provide in respect of typhoons was obscurely worded. If Ocean-routes intended to suspend positive routing advice in such conditions, that should have been much more clearly expressed."

I am familiar with the services provided by Ocean-routes. At the time of the *Derbyshire* loss, I was working as the operations' manager for a shipping company in Westport, Connecticut. We were operating a fleet of seven bulk carriers under time charter and employing them to carry cargoes that we had contracted with various shippers. We retained the services of Ocean-routes to monitor voyage performance by all the vessels under time charter to validate whether they were performing at the charter party speed the shipowners had warranted in the charter party agreement. Ocean-routes would assess the ships' performance against the prevailing weather and currents using their proprietary computer models. At the end of each voyage, they would send us a report that summarized the performance. The report would be used to establish that the ship had either performed or under-performed. In cases where there had been under-performance, the Ocean-routes report was used as the backup to support a performance claim. In my experience, this was the principal business of Ocean-routes. They earned fees for their services, meeting a need for post-voyage performance analysis on ships employed on a time charter basis.

By the mid-eighties, I was directly responsible for a fleet of over 20 bulk carriers all on time charter, and we employed the services of Ocean-routes as a principal means of carrying out post-voyage analysis. In reading Justice Colman's report, it is clear to me that he was of the understanding that Ocean-routes was engaged to act as a routing service or guide to masters. It is true that they provided information pre-voyage on the optimum route where choices exist to sail (for example, a great circle route, or a rhumb line, or a combination of both). On many routes, there are no such options, and Ocean-routes were primarily engaged to provide post-voyage analysis for the time charterer to evaluate charter party performance.

The late Professor Douglas Faulkner of the University of Glasgow was retained as one of the assessors to assist Lord Donaldson. Faulkner subsequently resigned from his role as an assessor for reasons unknown. However, Faulkner was an advocate for the existence of rogue or freak waves and believed this had been the primary cause of the *Derbyshire* being lost on September 10, 1980. Perhaps his belief in this theory placed him at odds with the other assessors. I do not know, but in 1980 rogue or freak waves were not widely believed to exist.

Professor Faulkner was the founding editor of the *Journal of Marine Structures*. Following Faulkner's death, the journal reported the following: "In 2001, Prof Faulkner published a report saying the ship [*Derbyshire*] had probably been hit by an unpredictable freak wave. His conclusion was a breakthrough in the understanding of such waves and their effect on the old generation of bulk carriers." Professor Faulkner presented his opinions at a keynote address at the IFREMER conference in 2000, titled "Rogue Waves—Defining Their

Characteristics for Marine Design." (IFREMER is the French institute that undertakes research and expert assessments to advance knowledge on the oceans and their resources, monitor the marine environment and foster the sustainable development of maritime activities.)

Professor Faulkner wrote the following in his keynote address at IFREMER.

3.2 Critical Ship Conditions

A provisional but not comprehensive list of ship design related subjects which have been suggested for Survival Design considerations includes:

(a) Primary hull strength
(b) Hatch cover and coaming strength
(c) Fore end protection
(d) Wave impact on hull and deck structure and fittings, and on bridge fronts
(e) Capsize, especially of small vessels
(f) Cargo shift, cargo damage
(g) Pooping damage
(h) Steering when hove to (inadequate rudder size)
(i) Hatchless container ships

The recommendations from the final DERBYSHIRE proceedings [8] should take care of (b) for forward hatch covers in large ships, because the principles of survival design are being applied. But, all hatch covers and coamings are vulnerable, and smaller cargo ships must be included. Of the remainder (a) and (d) are perhaps the most important and are now briefly discussed.

Primary Hull Strength.
Two independent dynamic simulations for the m.v. DERBYSHIRE and for an offshore FPSO typical of those now operating in the northern North Sea and west of Shetland have shown that maximum realistic wave induced bending moments in the hull girder could well exceed present requirements, perhaps by as much as:
- 40% in the hogging mode—
- 80% in the sagging mode.
This is clearly serious and should be investigated further. In the last four years a large container ship and a medium size bulk carrier have broken their backs, both were maintained in reasonable condition. Two badly maintained tankers broke their backs—the ERICA caused considerable pollution damage off the Brittany coast in October 1999. It is not unreasonable to assume that a first principles survival design approach, of the type illustrated above, would have provided an additional safety

margin to minimize if not eliminate such risks.

Professor Faulkner is a perfect example of the importance of dialog to ensure that there is greater awareness of understanding reality enabling ships to be designed and built that can genuinely weather the storm and be fit for the intended purpose. Note his reference (c) to fore end protection and (b) Hatch cover and coaming strength. There were latent defects in the design and construction of the *Derbyshire*. For many years there had been reports of rogue or freak waves, but the lack of evidence other than the testimony of professional mariners resulted in this dialog being suppressed as folklore and fiction. The *Derbyshire* may have met the standards for classification rules, but as we have seen all too often, when the standards are wrong, this is of no comfort to those who grieve the loss of their loved ones. Consequently, ships like the *Derbyshire* were under-designed to cope with the extreme conditions that exist at sea. Perhaps a forecastle to protect the ventilation pipes and stronger hatch covers would have prevented the need for the twenty-year campaign by the Derbyshire Families Association.

Four: Marine Electric, 1983

The last British ship I had sailed on had been an ore carrier called the *Finnamore Meadow*. The *Meadow* was on a long-term charter to British Steel shuttling around the Atlantic loading iron ore from Scandinavia, West Africa and Canada, to feed the British Steel blast furnaces in the UK. I joined the *Finnamore Meadow*, an ore carrier barely one-seventh the carrying capacity of the *Derbyshire*, in 1972, on a rainy night in March at the port of Immingham. The *Meadow* was popular because she was always trading to and from United Kingdom ports. Glasgow, Newport, Middlesbrough, and Immingham were our four principal destinations. Discharge was slow and typically took three to four days due to the older port facilities available in the 1970s. This gave the officers time to see their family on a regular basis. That was the positive argument.

As the weeks passed, I learned the darker side of the *Meadow*. The *Meadow* was a rust-bucket, and everyone knew that she leaked like a colander. I first noticed it while taking a draft reading on the dock at Newport. We had ballasted our side tanks and as I walked along the pier, I saw a stream of water coming from the ship's side—literally a hole in our hull plating through which the ballast was leaking out. I was shocked and reported it to the chief mate. This was old news to him, a regular on the *Meadow*. He merely said, "Well, we'll have to keep that tank topped up!" Ballast leaked from tank to tank, and from the tanks into the cargo hold and through the hull. I understood then why many would request leave if the *Meadow* got orders to cross the Atlantic to load ore in Canada. That meant battling against the North Atlantic in ballast, and they all knew that she was not in good shape. While at anchor waiting for cargo, the chief mate asked me to assist with an inspection of the #1 port ballast tank. After it had been opened up, we descended the ladder to the first level. I was shocked at what I observed. The level of corrosion was beyond anything I had ever seen. Large sections of steelwork were completely wasted away and had disappeared from view. We did not spend much time in that tank. I wondered how it could be that we remained in class with Lloyds and were considered seaworthy. But then I knew that many times when we prepared for an annual Load line or Safety survey the surveyor would disappear to the master's cabin for a few drinks and a chat, and we would magically receive our new certificates.

The final evidence came while we were anchored off Monrovia waiting for a cargo of Liberian iron ore. The chief engineer had decided he might weld the hull to stop the forepeak tank from leaking. So, we rigged staging over the bow and welding equipment was positioned. For several days there was a steady arc flash as the chief did his best to weld the cracks. Exasperated, he finally gave up and told me that as he welded a crack, a new break opened up before him. The heat from the welding caused the steel plate to fracture. He gave up his attempt to repair it.

The *Marine Electric* had been built in 1944 as a T2 tanker at the Sun Shipyard in Philadelphia. She was converted to a bulk carrier in 1962. The conversion gave the *Marine Electric* a new mid-body and moved her bridge aft. However, like the *Derbyshire,* she was not designed to have a forecastle, even though all T2 Tankers had this protection. The bow section of the T2 was welded to the new mid-body fabricated in Germany, and the main deck was then flush with the forecastle. It is possible that the molded depth of the hull cross-section had been increased to provide greater cubic capacity for steam coal. The salient fact is the *Marine Electric* had no protection of her foredeck hatch covers because there was no forecastle to buffer the effects of seas over her bow.

At the Marine Board of Inquiry, Bob Cusick, one of the three survivors, testified about the poor condition of the hatch covers. They had many holes due to wastage, and the crew were continually patching and repairing them. Cusick had made and submitted extensive reports to the master. At the Marine Board of Inquiry, Cusick was a lone voice testifying to the real condition of the *Marine Electric*. Captain Farnham, the regular master of the *Marine Electric*, chose to side with the owners Marine Transport Lines, denying that the ship was in such poor condition. Sadly, neither the Coast Guard nor the American Bureau of Shipping surveyors paid attention to the real conditions that existed before the loss. This convenient oversight enabled the *Marine Electric* to continue to be in class. The bow and the stern section of the *Marine Electric* were 39 years old, the mid-body 21 years old when she went down off Chincoteague, Virginia.

In his book *Until the Sea Shall Free Them*, Robert Frump tells the story of those final hours through the voice of Bob Cusick. In the early hours of February 12, 1983, Cusick knew that the *Marine Electric* was in trouble. She was down by the head when she should have been slightly trimmed by the stern. Cusick could only surmise that something had failed in the bow—perhaps the forepeak tank had flooded from a broken ventilation pipe. As discussed earlier, in 1983, there were no remote sensors for tanks and bilges. This was all measured manually, and nobody could go forward to take soundings during the storm and at that time of night.

The effect of being down by the head was that green seas were breaking over the bow and straight towards the frail hatch covers of number 1 hatch. Cusick knew that the many patches, the defective rubber seals and the missing dogs and cleats would mean that the hatch cover would collapse under the weight of those green seas. This was happening less than three years after the loss of the *Derbyshire*. Both ships suffered flooding in the bow area that caused their bow down condition, and neither ship had a forecastle to protect the forward hatch covers.

In many ways the story of my experience on the *Finnamore Meadow* parallels the *Marine Electric*. We all knew that our ships were frail, but we chose to remain silent and accepted the reality.

The crew of the *Marine Electric* were on a shuttle run carrying steam coal from Norfolk, Virginia to Boston, a routine run that took 36 hours in each direction and never left the coast by much distance. The *Finnamore Meadow* was on a shuttle run to fetch iron ore to feed the blast furnaces in the UK. However, the *Meadow* had one advantage over the *Marine Electric*: we had a forecastle that protected our hatch covers.

Another ship that I sailed on as chief mate was the *St Lawrence Prospector*. She was a bulk carrier of similar size to the *Marine Electric*, built in 1963 at the Short Brothers yard in Sunderland. She carried the name *Carlton* until being put under Canadian flag in 1975. The *Carlton* was designed as a Universal Bulk Carrier with a configuration of four upper and five lower cargo holds. However, she was designed with a robust forecastle which served to protect the hatch covers. The *Marine Electric* conversion took place in 1962, the *Carlton* was built new in 1963.

During my time onboard the *St Lawrence Prospector*, I encountered two situations which in retrospect I now realize we came very close to that final hole in the Swiss Cheese Model. The first was challenging for me because I was sent to join the *Prospector* having just been issued my Canadian first mate's license. I joined at a grain elevator in the lower St Lawrence where the ship was loading wheat bound for Halifax, Nova Scotia. The chief mate onboard only had an Inland Waters certificate, so he was not licensed to be out in the Atlantic. He was not familiar with the grain loading regulations that require detailed calculations on the stability and free surface of the grain. As I stepped onboard, I was thrust straight into discussions with the Department of Transport surveyor who would be verifying that the ship met the regulations for the planned voyage.

The challenge was that there were two parcels of different grain that had to be segregated, and the stowage factor and arrangement would result in two holds partially filled. The free surface resulting from these partially filled holds had to be calculated to ensure that we had adequate stability to remain within the regulations. The key was that to sail in this condition the filled holds had to be full, with no void spaces. I would be acceptable to have untrimmed ends, but the sides had to contain no voids. As I watched the loading, I became concerned the wings were not being filled. During a break in the loading, I inspected one of the holds and discovered the grain was not flowing into the space below the wing tanks. I was worried. We might have been able to demonstrate on paper a set of calculations that looked satisfactory, but I knew that the voids in the wings could allow grain to shift during rolling, and this would have important consequences. I spoke to the master and explained my concerns. He listened, and a few hours later, I was summoned to the dock office to talk to the marine superintendent at head office. They wanted to understand my concern. I explained and suggested that the only solution would be to hire a gang of trimmers to fill the voids manually. This suggestion did not go over well. I was told this was impossible, and I would just have to find a way to sort it out. As we finished the loading, I pleaded with the stevedores to get as much grain into the wings as they could using their automatic trimmer. It was at least something, I thought. I completed the regulatory paperwork with the Canadian government surveyor, and on paper we were okay— close to the margin, but acceptable. I knew different, and even though I was a young, first-trip mate, my intuition told me that the sooner we got to Halifax the better.

The voyage to the port of Halifax requires passage through the Gulf of St Lawrence, and then you pass into the Atlantic via the Cabot Strait. In the space of a few miles, you leave the tranquil waters of the Gulf of St Lawrence, sheltered by Cape Breton Island, Newfoundland and Prince Edward Island, and enter into the turbulence of the Atlantic Ocean, and the conflicting currents of cold water from Labrador and the warm water of the Gulf Stream. Beneath the Cabot Strait lies the Laurentian Trough, a deep gouge created by glacial ice that forms a deep channel between the Atlantic and the Gulf of St Lawrence.

The seas in the area above the Laurentian Trough are often exaggerated as the energy of the Atlantic is squeezed into this narrow space. To reach the port of Halifax requires leaving the deep water of the Cabot Strait and turning to starboard, crossing over the Scotian shelf, a shallow section of the Atlantic. I knew that our most vulnerable moment would be making that turn: if we rolled excessively, the grain might shift, and once it did, we would develop a list. As we made the transition out of the Cabot Strait, I held my breath. I had not slept well since we completed loading. I felt the heavy burden on my shoulders, and a little voice in my head reminded me that if this went wrong, I would be responsible. This was the summer of 1975, a few months before the *Edmund Fitzgerald* would be lost on Lake Superior. We survived intact and made it safely into Halifax. I breathed and slept again.

On the second voyage, we loaded grain for a North Atlantic crossing to Oslo, Norway. I made sure that all my holds were well trimmed and filled to capacity because a November voyage across the North Atlantic required our ship to be in good condition. What I did not know until we arrived in Oslo was that we had developed a crack on the main deck from the hatch coaming by way of number three hold. The crack went from the hatch coaming across the deck like a snake. The grain inside the hold was wet and damaged by sea water. In the hold, a stalagmite of damaged grain led downwards from the crack to the bottom of the hold. I stood on the deck studying that crack and realizing how lucky we were to have arrived safely. I left the ship in Oslo and was re-assigned to a Panamax self-unloading bulk carrier waiting for me at the dry-dock in Hamburg, Germany. A few years later the fore-body of the *Prospector* was scrapped, and a new hull was attached to the old engine room. We were on the North Atlantic when the *Edmund Fitzgerald* went down on Lake Superior.

I first read Robert Frump's book about the *Marine Electric* in 2002, shortly after it was published. I was fortunate to meet Bob, and he signed my copy of *Until the Sea Shall Free Them*. I introduced Bob as a special guest at the annual dinner of the Seamen's Church Institute, the seafarer mission that has served the needs of seafarers on the Delaware River since 1843. Bob wrote the following: "*To David, Thank you for kind words and hospitality. Readers like you make this a great joy. Very Best, Bob Frump.*" I was impressed by the quality of his writing and his understanding of the life of a merchant seafarer and the business of shipping. Not all writers who choose to write about maritime disasters take the time to understand the terminology or the culture. Much of what Bob Frump wrote about regarding the *Marine Electric* reflects the challenge of the right dialog that would have prevented the activation of the latent defects that shifted a routine voyage into the final journey. In the *Marine Electric*, we see the template for what would happen to another American merchant ship the *El Faro* in 2015. Why were the lessons of the *Marine Electric* not implemented? Both the *Marine Electric* and the *El Faro* were of a similar age when

71

they went down. They were both built at the same shipyard. They both had regular shuttle runs and were in constant view of the Coast Guard.

The three people who survived the sinking of the *Marine Electric* had different paths to rescue. Bob Cusick the chief mate found the port lifeboat. Before the capsize he had been getting the starboard lifeboat ready to launch. The starboard lifeboat had been damaged when the *Marine Electric* went down rolling over on her starboard side. The port lifeboat had broken free and this provided sanctuary for Bob Cusick. Cusick's greatest challenge was how to get onboard the lifeboat. This is no easy task when you are in the water fully clothed. Cusick managed to roll himself into the boat using the natural motion of the waves. The new insulated coat Bob's wife Bea had purchased Cusick provided him protection from hypothermia. During that night Cusick held on as the lifeboat was tossed around and kept his mind focused on the Coast Guard coming to the rescue. This mindfulness is reminiscent of Colin Armitage's 50-day ordeal in a lifeboat in 1943 after his ship the *Lulworth Hill* was sunk by a torpedo. Colin spent every day expecting a rescue ship, and Bob Cusick remained focused on the Coast Guard showing up while singing his favorite song. At daybreak, it was a Norwegian tanker the *Barranger* that discovered Bob Cusick. The challenge then was how to transfer Bob from his lifeboat to the safety of the *Barranger*.

Regretfully, all the *Barranger* could do was to radio the Coast Guard and request their help. Both Cusick and the master of the *Barranger* knew that they had no safe way to retrieve Cusick under those sea conditions. Coast Guard helicopter 1471 was low on fuel, but they had a winch and a basket. They responded to the *Barranger*'s call and went to rescue Cusick from his lifeboat. Onboard CG 1471 were seven dead bodies. They lowered the basket to the lifeboat, and on the third attempt, Cusick rolled into it. The Coast Guard now had Bob Cusick and winched him to safety.

Dewey, the able seaman, found a life-raft and managed to get into it after 20 minutes. Others who were in the frigid water and suffering the effects of hypothermia tried but could not, and Dewey was alone in the raft as one by one the others succumbed to the cold. A US Navy helicopter with a Navy diver onboard sighted the canopy of Dewey's life-raft and lowered their rescue basket. Dewey rolled in and was soon onboard the chopper.

Eugene Kelly, the relief third mate, found a life ring he had thrown overboard and was sharing with five others. One by one the others succumbed to hypothermia. Jim McCann, the Navy diver, was busy working in the water placing the bodies he found into the basket to be lifted aboard the helicopter. McCann discovered Kelly, and he was the only one still clinging to the life ring he had thrown overboard. Kelly joined Dewey onboard the Coast Guard helicopter

Only three survived, and each by a different means. The story of their rescue highlights not only the incredible challenge for merchant mariners to escape their ship safely but the challenge of being picked up safely. A helicopter rescue is limited by the range of the helicopter, so this is fine when you are near the coast. However, if you are mid-ocean and need to be picked by a rescue ship, it is dangerous and complicated to make the transfer, especially if those to be retrieved are in poor health or injured. When Colin Armitage and Ken Cooke were finally rescued by a Royal Navy destroyer, they could not climb up a net to safety. They were too frail after 50 days in a lifeboat. The Royal Navy sailors had to climb down and carry them. This is fine when sea conditions are calm. Another issue that remains a challenge for the newer enclosed lifeboats, which can rapidly stern launch on a sliding rail, is how do you safely get out of the enclosed lifeboats and rescued by a passing ship?

Consider the following questions. When the *Marine Electric* was converted, did Marine Transport Lines consider having a new bow section built with a raised forecastle that would protect the foredeck hatches? By retaining the 20-year-old bow from the T2 tanker, they were setting up a latent defect. Why were the marine superintendents blind to the condition of their own vessel? How could they not question why the chief mate was ordering so much Red Hand fiberglass bonding? Did they inquire what it was for? (In my day at sea with British shipowners, if you ordered an extra set of 2B pencils for the chart room, questions would be asked.)

Where were the regulatory officials, the Coast Guard, the classification society surveyors? Did they actively choose not to see and not to observe? Sadly, this is a perversion of trust not unique to the Maritime industry. In recent events like the Grenfell fire in London and the Brumadinho Dam collapse in Brazil, we have seen there has been a convenient diversion of oversight from those who are charged with acting responsibly but fail to do so because they are swayed by other influences. I experienced this when I made the decision to sail the *St Lawrence Prospector* with a cargo of grain at risk of shifting, and Bob Cusick did it when he left Norfolk with hatch covers riddled with patches. What differentiates outcomes in instances where individuals have to bear responsibility for such situations where latent defects are at play are the individual actions the individuals take in that moment. If you are aware of the latent defect, you may not be able to change it, but you may be able to mitigate its effect. In my case, I made a valiant effort to trim the cargo holds as full as I could, and I made sure that we were very careful when we altered course off Nova Scotia. These actions may have functioned as mitigation.

For Bob Cusick, the latent defects could not be mitigated to save the *Marine Electric*. However, Bob Cusick devoted himself to telling the real story before the Marine Board of Inquiry and in so doing his dialog brought forward the evidence that might otherwise have been suppressed. Robert Frump reports a meeting that Bob Cusick had with the port chaplain Cliff Olsen in Norfolk before the Marine Board of Inquiry hearing. Olsen said the following: *"Don't go looking for a pillar of fire or a burning bush here, Bob. There is a reason you were saved. There is an answer to why. If you are not seeing it 'out there,' then look inside. The answer is inside. It is within you. You will know the reason. When the time comes that God wants you to see the reason, you will know it."* This "Look within" made sense. Frump wrote about Cusick, "He decided he would not hem and haw and say, 'I don't recall' at the hearing. He would not be a crusader either… He would simply say what was in his heart and mind."

At the Marine Board of Inquiry, there were three Coast Guard officers. One would become the champion to navigate the hearings and to press for change following the findings. His name was Captain Domenic A. Calicchio. Unlike the chairman and the other member, Calicchio had the benefit of 23 years of experience in the Merchant Marine sailing as a master. During the hearings, it was Calicchio who asked the questions that upset the testimony of expert witnesses. These were witnesses who had been retained by Marine Transport Lines to put forward other reasons for the loss to divert attention away from the poor condition of the hatch covers. Calicchio campaigned for the commandant of the Coast Guard to issue sweeping changes. He did not succeed because the changes were only partially approved by the commandant. The two key findings not supported were to remove the American Bureau of Shipping from their role of ship inspection, and to replace the Coast Guard's role in inspections with a new agency manned by experienced merchant mariners. Calicchio succeeded in the creation of the Coast Guard rescue swimmer program, regulations for survival suits to be onboard, and the fitting of emergency beacons.

The Coast Guard did carry out enhanced inspections in the years immediately following the loss of the *Marine Electric*. In 2003, Domenic Calicchio was posthumously given the Plimsoll award by the *Professional Mariner* magazine. In 2015, the largest US Merchant Marine casualty would take place with the loss of the *El Faro* during Hurricane Joaquim.

The failings of the out-sourced inspections carried out by the American Bureau of Shipping and insufficient oversight by the Coast Guard reverberated back to the campaign by Captain Domenic Calicchio to bring about change. Calicchio's efforts to bring that dialog forward were a valiant effort to do the right thing. Robert Frump wrote that Calicchio had written a letter of reply to Lisolette Fredette, the mother of a mariner lost onboard another American ship the *Poet*. Lisolette wrote to Calicchio to thank him for being so persistent and critical at the *Marine Electric* hearings. In his reply Calicchio wrote, "*However, any investigative report regardless of its completeness and soundness, aside from good reading, has little or no value, unless immediate action is taken to implement reasonable and sound recommendations made by the board to prevent a repetition.*"

Calicchio reveals in this letter his compassion for the merchant mariner. During such hearings the legal teams are sparring to avoid liability. Their focus is not on exposing cause to learn how a future event can be prevented. Calicchio demonstrated he would not entertain false theories that would allow anyone to shield themselves from responsibility. Calicchio's focus was on finding the root cause and then bringing about the change that would prevent it from happening again. During my commercial career, I have served as the chair and co-chair of two industrial accident inquiries, and at the outset, we make it clear that our task was to reveal the root cause so that learning could be achieved, and positive change effected. This is the right form of dialog that needs to happen.

Five: Herald of Free Enterprise, 1987

On the evening of March 6, 1987, the British ferry *Herald of Free Enterprise* capsized in the Belgian port of Zeebrugge. The result would be the loss of 193 lives and a wake-up call for the safe operation of roll-on roll-off ferries. At the formal investigation led by Mr. Justice Sheen serving in the capacity of wreck commissioner from April 27, 1987, to June 12, 1987, Mr. Justice Sheen and his team of four assessors considered all the evidence and found as follows:

> "The Court, having carefully inquired into the circumstances attending the above-mentioned shipping casualty, finds, for the reasons stated in the Report, that the capsizing of the *HERALD OF FREE ENTERPRISE* was partly caused or contributed to by serious negligence in the discharge of their duties by Captain David Lewry (Master), Mr. Leslie Sabel (Chief Officer) and Mr. Mark Victor Stanley (Assistant bosun), and partly caused **or** contributed to by the fault of Townsend Car Ferries Limited (the Owners). The court suspends the certificate of the said Captain David Lewry for a period of one year from the 24, July 1987. The Court suspends the

certificate of the said Mr. Leslie Sabel for a period of two years from the 24, July 1987."

Mr. Justice Sheen's report detailed failures that revealed a broken chain of dialog that led from the individual who should have closed the bow door all the way to the senior management of the owners, Townsend Car Ferries, then part of the P&O Ferries group. There were latent defects that existed in the design of the ferry that would have been simple and relatively inexpensive to address when the ferry was built. Indicators on the navigating bridge that would have displayed the status of the watertight doors at the bow and the stern were not fitted. Simple warning devices could have been interlocked to ensure that the bridge team would always be fully aware and could neither open the watertight doors before docking or leave without closing. Instead, Townsend Car Ferries had focused their time and resources on speed and style and missed a critical safety item—making sure their ferry was not vulnerable to capsize.

The *Herald of Free Enterprise* led to significant changes in UK law and the introduction of the Corporate Manslaughter and Corporate Homicide Act in 2007.

In 2007, I served as a senior manager with Corus, the Anglo-Dutch steel company. In May 2007, I attended the Corus annual senior managers conference held in London. The gathering of some

400 managers spent an entire day of the two-day session focused on Process Safety and the introduction of the new Corporate Manslaughter Act and Corporate Homicide Act, which received Royal Assent on July 26, 2007, and would be in effect from April 6, 2008. The CEO of Corus Philippe Varin was deeply committed to safety, and during his time at the helm of this global steel operation, he made a strong commitment to changing the culture to ensure that safety was always at the forefront of every action. Varin was appointed the chief executive of Corus in May 2003. Varin took the helm at Corus with a challenging financial situation for the business and dark clouds looming as a result of a major explosion at the Port Talbot steelworks in Wales during November 2001. Three steelworkers died at blast furnace number 5, and in 2007, following the investigations, Corus was fined the sum of £1,200,000 and ordered to pay costs for its breach of health and safety laws. A report by Reuters News stated the following:

> "During the hearing, Corus pleaded guilty in respect of our failings under the Health and Safety at Work Act," board member Rauke Henstra said:

> "We have always maintained that an explosion of this type and magnitude that

occurred was neither foreseen nor was it foreseeable and this has been accepted by the prosecution," he said in a statement.

The Health and Safety Executive, which brought the prosecution, said the fine was "insignificant" compared with the grief of the dead men's families.

"This was systematic corporate management failure at the Port Talbot works. Proper management attention may have broken the chain which led to the explosion," said Terry Rose, the head of the Health and Safety Executive in Wales.

On April 25, 2006, another steel worker died at the Port Talbot steel works. Corus was fined £500,000 plus costs by the Swansea Court. The Health and Safety Inspector stated the following:

HSE Principal Inspector Colin Mew revealed the company had a reporting system, which showed a significant number of near-misses where steam had led to dangerous situations. He also explained that the firm should have installed barriers around the open channel.

"The lack of visibility caused by steam and the open channel were a fatal combination, which should have been foreseen by the company," said Principal Inspector Mew.

"This horrific incident could have been avoided if the company had a system in place to ensure that either no covers were left off the channel or, if they needed to be left off, a temporary barrier was erected around them."

Kevin Downey died following the incident at blast furnace 4 in 2006. Downey had been actively involved in the rescue of his colleagues during the 2001 explosion at blast furnace 5.

I joined Corus in December 2005 as the supply chain director at the Teesside steelworks, notable for having the largest blast furnace in the United Kingdom and the second largest in Europe. In April, I was sent to attend a week-long Safety course being held for senior managers at the Dutch steelworks in Ijmuiden. I was seated in a group that included the managing director of the Port Talbot steelworks. The April 25, 2006, accident that killed Kevin Downey occurred while we were on the course and the managing director had to leave at short notice to attend the aftermath of the accident.

Making steel is a hazardous activity that involves high pressures and temperatures. Simply put, it is the business of cooking rocks to release the pure iron separating the rock by heating it to a temperature where it becomes molten. The iron is denser and can, therefore, be tapped and drained into ladles—this becomes what is known as pig iron. That is the primary process of a blast furnace. This is where the two Port Talbot accidents happened.

Safety has two elements. Process Safety is the system of managing unintentional releases of hazardous chemicals, energy or any other material. Behavioral or Occupational Safety is the management of the interface between people and process. Process Safety can affect a large group of individuals when a major incident occurs, whereas Behavioral or Occupational Safety typically affects small groups or individuals.

In the case of the *Herald of Free Enterprise*, the observer could be drawn to focus on the failure of the assistant bosun to close the watertight doors as a Behavioral Safety failing, but upon a more holistic investigation, it is clear the capsize of the ferry at Zeebrugge was actually a Process Safety failure. There was a systemic fault that allowed the latent defects to be built into the operation of the ferry. The assistant bosun certainly was the individual who interfaced with the "Process," but he was not the architect of the system—a system which was not connected to ensure that the primary decision-makers would know whether the watertight doors were open or closed during a time when the ship had been ballasted down by the head to accommodate the shore ramp at Zeebrugge.

In his book *A Life in Error*, Professor James Reason said the following concerning the *Herald of Free Enterprise*:

> "There was a lot going on in the real world. The distinction between active and latent failures owes a great deal to Mr. Justice Sheen's observations regarding the capsize of the Herald of Free Enterprise in 1987. He wrote: 'At first sight the faults which led to the disaster were the... errors of commission on the part of the Master, the Chief Officer and the assistant bosun... But a full investigation into the circumstances of the disaster led inexorably to the conclusion that the underlying or cardinal faults lay higher up in the Company... From top to bottom the body corporate was infected with the disease of sloppiness.'"

In short, the Herald was a 'sick' ship even before it sailed from Zeebrugge on 6 March 1987. The latent failures included:

• Low-capacity ballast pumps that were insufficient to out the vessel on an even keel in less than half the voyage time. Request for higher-capacity pumps had been rejected.

• Despite repeated warnings, there were no remote bridge indicators to detect and warn of open bow doors.

• The vessel had a chronic list to port. This, together with the inadequacy of the scuppers and the high center of gravity, made it inevitable that the ship would turn turtle rapidly and catastrophically.

• Inadequate checking of the number of passengers aboard. Numbers had exceeded passenger limits on several prior occasions.

• Poor storage and design of lifejackets. Tangled masses of floating lifejackets prevented some swimmers from reaching the surface.

• High crew workload due to under-manning and poor tasking.

• Low morale due to poor working conditions and longstanding disputes between seafarers and land-based management.

• Company procedures that were both ambiguous and inappropriate.

• Safety issues were subordinated to those of productivity and cost-cutting in a wide range of activities.

• A culture that condoned (or rendered unavoidable) violations of safe operating procedures.

"The distinction between active and latent failures rests upon two considerations: first, the length of time before the failures have a bad outcome; second, where in the organization the failures occur. Generally, active failures are committed by those in direct contact with the system and have an immediate though often short-lived impact; latent failures occur within the higher echelons of the company, and their adverse effects may be delayed by many years."

Mr. Justice Sheen's report highlighted the fact that there had been repeated incidences of proceeding to sea with bow or stern doors open (section 12.5, page 12) and that the system which was in operation on all the Spirit class vessels was defective (section 12.6, page 13). In section 13.3 Sheen wrote, "Captain Kirby [the senior master] ought to have applied his mind to the contents of those [standing] orders. If he had done so, he would certainly have appreciated their defects. Captain Kirby was one of many masters who failed to apply their minds to those orders and to take steps to have them clarified.

Here we see a reference to the concept of "individual mindfulness" a term described by Professor James Reason in his book, *Organizational Accidents Revisited*. Reason defines "individual mindfulness" as the actions at the local level. While this is an essential ingredient, it cannot succeed without the benefit of "collective mindfulness" the systemic process that acts to support and sustain it. Sheen describes the lack of "collective mindfulness" within Townsend Car Ferries. In section 14, Sheen wrote, "The Board of Directors did not appreciate their responsibility for the safe management of their ships. They did not apply their minds to the question: What orders should be given for the safety of our ships? The directors did not have any proper comprehension of what their duties were." Sheen's report detailed the failure of the "collective mindfulness" to support and sustain the crews tasked with operating the Spirit class ferries. In section 16, page 17, Sheen wrote, "But the real complaint, which appears to the Court to be fully justified, was that the 'Marine Department' did not listen to the complaints or suggestions or wishes of their Masters."

Regarding the repeated request by masters for a mimic indicator on the bridge to display the status of the bow and stern doors, these requests can be seen as the desire of the "individual mindfulness," but unless the "collective mindfulness" of the management listened and acted, no action would take place. Sheen picked up on this in section 18, page 25 when he wrote: "That it was simple was illustrated by the fact within a matter of days after the disaster indicator lights were installed in the remaining Spirit class ships and other ships of the fleet."

I witnessed the phenomenon of "individual mindfulness" and the interface with "collective mindfulness" during my time at sea. In one example, I had joined the *Phosphore Conveyor*, a Panamax self-unloading bulk carrier under extensive repair at a shipyard in Hamburg. The ship had suffered crankshaft failures on both of her main engines due to insufficient lubrication and the latent defect of both engines sharing a single sump. One engine failed and shortly after, so did the second.

The *Phosphore Conveyor* was only five years old at the time and had to be towed across the Atlantic to Germany to await two new crankshafts being made and fitted. The ship was jointly owned by US and Canadian owners and was registered in Liberia. The management of the ship had been contracted out to a third-party manager who employed a crew made up of European officers with ratings from Barbados. Following the catastrophic engine failure and a review of the poor operating history, the owners made a decision to take the management of the ship in-house. The Canadian owner agreed to take over the management and supply the officers, the

Barbados ratings would remain. I joined the ship about two months before the repairs would be completed and used that time to learn about the past problems by listening to the bosun from Barbados. In its entire five years of operation, this sophisticated self-unloader had yet to make a successful self-unload of a single cargo. Each time they would attempt to discharge they would fail, for various reasons. I had served on Canadian flag belt-type self-unloaders, and as I studied the ship, I saw no reason why a self-discharge could not be accomplished.

During the transition, the marine superintendent from the prior management company remained in attendance at the shipyard to complete the extensive repairs. A key safety aspect of any belt-type self-unloader are the watertight doors in the belt-tunnel that need to be closed at sea to ensure that there is watertight integrity at each bulkhead between the ship's cargo holds. The marine superintendent had been responsible for the ship for the prior years, and he was not pleased with the fact that his firm was being replaced. We were onboard to take over the ship, but the official handover would not happen until all the repairs had been completed. During this transition period, as chief officer, I made several requests for inspections and checks. One of these was to observe the watertight doors in operation. The marine superintendent initially balked at my request as unnecessary and a waste of his time. I stood my ground and insisted it was a major safety issue and I would not accept unless they had been tested.

We assembled in the belt-tunnel—the doors were hydraulically operated from a lever in the walkway on the aft side. Doors would be closed in sequence from forward to aft, and then the operator would follow the belt-tunnel up through the transfer bay to the main deck. There was a mimic panel on the bridge. As we stood grouped around the door, the operator moved the control handle, but neither the upper nor lower section of the watertight doors moved. Instead, they pulsed and vibrated in position. This caused the marine superintendent to become agitated, and he tried the control lever himself, with the same result. He then explained there must be a fault, and we moved to the next set of doors. We observed the same result. On that day, none of the watertight doors worked. The reason was simple: the hydraulic hoses had been fitted in reverse, and so when the control lever was actuated the cylinders tried to open rather than close—this was why they pulsed and vibrated. We had just witnessed a perfect example of a failure of "collective mindfulness": the system was at fault and had been so for some time. I do not know if they ever had been closed. My "individual mindfulness" had challenged the system, and the simple demonstration proved the point. During my six months serving on the ship, we successfully self-discharged several cargoes of ore and phosphate rock, much to the great surprise of the shore terminals who believed the ship was jinxed.

During my time working at Corus, I observed the passionate efforts of the CEO Philippe Varin to inject a culture of safety into a large corporate structure engaged in an extremely hazardous business of cooking rocks. Varin brought in safety consultants and embarked on a major training exercise across the entire organization. The 2001 explosion at Port Talbot had not been on his watch, but the investigation and the eventual findings would be revealed under his tenure. He therefore knew that action could not wait until the completion of the investigation. Under Varin's leadership, all the senior executive team were engaged in conducting safety audits at the plant level. This included Varin himself, and when these took place it was handled without the typical pomp and circumstance of a "royal" visit. When Varin came to visit a section of our steelworks, he would meet the local managing director, but the actual site tour would take place with the area manager on a one-on-one basis with Varin. Varin liked to engage with workers on the floor and would ask them two questions: What do you do to make this safer? What do you need to make it better? In my experience, few CEOs are willing to engage with the workforce in the way that Varin did. Each month of the year, we would see one of the executive level team touring some part of the Teesside steelworks. This system of engagement trickled down throughout the organization. As a member of the local business team, I also conducted safety audits within other areas of the Teesside plant. Several times a year we held week-long sessions where we would engage directly with the shift workers in briefing sessions. I would brief small groups of about 20 workers in 90-minute sessions, and this would go through the night at two-hour intervals. All this was designed to improve communication, increase awareness and ensure management remained in close contact with the front line of operations. In my own area of activity, we had an excellent safety record despite all the risk involved with the movement of liquid iron and heavy steel slabs. There was a high degree of man and machine interface, especially in the logistics of handling millions of tons around the clock.

The form of safety dialog Varin preached at Corus was clearly lacking within Townsend Car Ferries. If the senior executives had engaged directly with their operating teams on the ferries, they would have learned about some of the latent defects. However, they chose to abdicate their responsibility and remained aloof and disconnected.

During my time at Corus, I was asked to chair and co-chair two accident investigations. I chaired one involving an injury to a manager who was struck from behind by a vehicle while walking to his car at the parking lot near his office. The other, which I co-chaired, involved a derailment of a loaded torpedo ladle railcar carrying molten iron. Both of these investigations provided valuable insight into the realm of Process Safety. The forensics also revealed the importance of the detail work that needs to be done to accurately reconstruct the sequence of events and thereby expose the root cause. Mr. Justice Sheen and his team were very thorough in the work that they did concerning the root cause behind the capsize of the ferry and the loss of 193 lives. Anyone who finds themselves charged with the responsibility of investigation must adhere to finding the truth wherever that path may lead.

In my first case, the matter of the injured manager who had been struck from behind by another vehicle initially seemed to be an unfortunate case of the driver being distracted. The incident took place within the company site on private roads. The manager had left his office and was walking along the side of the road—there was no pavement for pedestrians. The time was in the late afternoon/evening, and it was winter, so it was dark. The manager did not park his car in the parking lot directly opposite his office, he preferred another parking lot further away. The company had published a set of cardinal site safety rules and these incorporated the UK Highway Code. Under the

Highway Code, when there is no pavement, pedestrians are required to always walk on the side of the road so that they face the oncoming traffic. The manager when walking to his car had walked on the left, with his back to the traffic passing closest to him, thereby violating the company rules. When this point was raised at the first hearing, the manager was indignant: he was still angry about the injury, and firmly of the belief that the driver was entirely at fault. When we interviewed the driver, he said, "I never saw him until he landed on the bonnet [hood] of my car."

Reviewing the evidence, it became clear to me that we were missing something. A few weeks later, I was driving my own car, and a pedestrian appeared from nowhere. It was a dark night, and the pedestrian was wearing dark clothes. This caused me to research camouflage and to check what clothing the manager had been wearing. The manager had dark pants and a dark jacket on when he was struck from behind. To prove the circumstance, I set about creating a reconstruction of the event. We simulated the time of day, the cloud cover, the state of the moon and then re-enacted the scene taking video from the car to establish the apparent view of the driver. This reconstruction showed that the manager, when walking with dark clothes with his back to the car, had no reflective capability and the immediate background was a dark set of structures, so the manager did not create a silhouette in any way. He just vanished from view. Therefore, the driver was correct. He could not discern the manager walking by the side of the road. Consequently, we found the root causes were: 1. Failure to observe the Highway Code and therefore a breach of company rules. 2. Failure by the company to establish safe walking corridors to and from the parking areas. 3. Failure by the company to require the wearing of a Hi-Viz PPE for pedestrians walking within the site (cyclists were already required to wear Hi-Viz, but pedestrians had been overlooked).

In the first instance, this investigation looked like a Behavioral Safety issue due to distracted driving. In reality, however, it was a Process Safety issue that had not adequately segregated man and machine.

In May 2007 when we gathered at the senior managers conference, Varin had arranged for a special focus on Process Safety. We were addressed by senior executives from BP. BP had recently experienced a major incident at their Texas City Oil Refinery in the USA. Fifteen people had died, and 180 been injured. BP used the Texas City findings to preach to us about the importance of Process Safety. At the time this was somewhat odd considering that BP had been found to have serious safety culture deficiencies at Texas City. In November 2007 BP would plead guilty to the 2006 Prudhoe Bay oil spill in Alaska. Subsequently, in

2010, BP was in major trouble when the Deepwater Horizon oil spill led to the resignation of their CEO and massive fines and costs. In some respects, perhaps an address by a company itself experiencing the negative effects of Process Safety might have been a wake-up call. I do recall the dialog that went on at our conference table: everyone agreed that Process Safety was terrific, and that we were all onboard, but we were unsure whether we would receive the funding to make all the changes that were needed.

The March 2007 report by the US Chemical and Investigation Board stated:

> "On March 23, 2005, at 1:20 p.m., the BP Texas City Refinery suffered one of the worst industrial disasters in recent US history. Explosions and fires killed 15 people and injured another 180, alarmed the community, and resulted in financial losses exceeding $1.5 billion. The incident occurred during the startup of an isomerization (ISOM) unit when a raffinate splitter tower was overfilled; pressure relief devices opened, resulting in a flammable liquid geyser from a blowdown stack that was not equipped with a flare. The release of flammables led to an explosion and fire. All of the fatalities occurred in or near office

trailers located close to the blowdown drum. A shelter-in-place order was issued that required 43,000 people to remain indoors. Houses were damaged as far away as three-quarters of a mile from the refinery.

"The BP Texas City facility is the third-largest oil refinery in the United States. Prior to 1999, Amoco owned the refinery. BP merged with Amoco in 1999 and BP subsequently took over operation of the plant."

"The Texas City disaster was caused by organizational and safety deficiencies at all levels of the BP Corporation. Warning signs of a possible disaster were present for several years, but company officials did not intervene effectively to prevent it. The extent of the serious safety culture deficiencies was further revealed when the refinery experienced two additional serious incidents just a few months after the March 2005 disaster. In one, a pipe failure caused a reported $30 million in damage; the other resulted in a $2 million property loss. In each incident, community shelter-in-place orders were issued."

My second panel of inquiry at Teesside involved many months of investigation. At our initial session, we had over 30 people present representing all the work streams connected with the movement of molten iron. I co-chaired with one of the plant engineers, an excellent engineer, and we worked well together as we looked for the root cause.

The molten iron was transported by rail from underneath the blast furnace along a dedicated rail line about four miles to the steel shop converters and casters. Special railcars known as torpedo cars carried a steel ladle that could rotate to pour the iron out at the steel shop. The inner side of the steel ladle contained refractory bricks to insulate the molten iron and to protect the steel casing. The torpedo cars were designed to carry 350 tons of molten iron, and when empty they weighed 350 tons. The route of the rail line required the plant locomotives to pull two loaded torpedoes up an incline and then over three bridges before descending towards the steelworks. The three bridges were as follows: first over the network railway line, second over the entrance road to the Corus site, and third over many chemical pipelines serving the nearby petrochemical industries. At the blast furnace, the rail tracks ran underneath the base of the furnace, and molten iron was tapped from the furnace and poured into the opening at the top of the torpedo.

The level of molten iron was controlled by the blast furnace operators observing the level. Before leaving the blast furnace, each torpedo was filled to an ullage aided by using a sensor that measured the level of molten iron. However, the actual fill varied depending on the skill of the operator and the timing of the closing the flow into the torpedo. After leaving the blast furnace, insulated lids were placed on top of the filling hole to retain the heat. Then the torpedo should have passed over a scale on the rail track; however, the scale had failed many years before and had never been repaired or replaced. So, for some years the torpedo cars went on their rail journey without check weighing. The axles, refractories and general repair of the torpedoes were made at the torpedo repair shop. During the investigation we discovered there was a serious ongoing problem of cracked axles and cracked sub-frames. The connection between these facts and overloading had not been made. Since there were no weights because the scale was broken, this was all unknown. When the derailed torpedo had to be lifted to replace the damaged sub-frames and axle assemblies, special heavy capacity mobile cranes were called in. Their first question was, "How much does this weigh?" In truth, nobody knew—so the best guess estimate was given. The crane operators rigged up and could not lift the torpedo. They had sophisticated load sensors on the cranes, and they reported the torpedo was far heavier than the estimate. They would need a larger crane. The torpedo was overloaded beyond the safe working limit.

Throughout the investigation, we found there had been a systemic failure of the "collective mindfulness" to fully appreciate the risks of moving overloaded torpedo cars containing molten iron on a route which had exposure to the public and the community. The site was governed by the UK COMAH rules, or Control of Major Accident Hazards, and clearly, the transport of molten iron by rail over three bridges used by the public and the community fell within the scope of COMAH.

Mr. Justice Sheen made reference to the importance of proceeding without delay. Sheen wrote: "An investigation into the causes of a casualty has the result that lessons are learned, which may make for greater safety in the future, then the sooner those lessons are learned, the better for the whole community." At Corus, after the first round of hearings, we immediately issued advice to increase the ullage of molten iron inside the torpedoes, thereby decreasing the weight carried. The most significant outcome was the decision to install a new rail scale system equipped with automated traffic lights that showed the locomotive drivers if it was safe to proceed. In an overload, the torpedo would have to be decanted at the nearby ore ponds before being weighed again and allowed to travel the route.

The *Herald of Free Enterprise* was salvaged by the Dutch company Smit-Tak Towage and Salvage. By the end of April the ferry was refloated and moved into Zeebrugge harbor and then to the De Schelde shipyard in Flushing so that the remaining bodies could be recovered. After repairs, attempts were made to sell the ship, but no buyers were found, and the ship was sold for scrapping in Taiwan. Renamed the *Flushing Range* and with the Townsend Thoresen markings painted over, she began her journey under tow to Kaohsiung, Taiwan. The journey to the breakers yard was an event in itself. In the Bay of Biscay, the towline parted, and while passing South Africa, the hull began to fail, requiring emergency repairs at Port Elizabeth before completing the journey to Kaohsiung.

The Townsend Thoresen brand name was forever tarnished by the loss of the *Herald of Free Enterprise*, and P&O Ferries rebranded under the name of P&O European Ferries with a new blue livery. The two sister ships continued operating in their new color scheme. The *Spirit of Free Enterprise* was scrapped in 2012 and the *Pride of Free Enterprise* in 2015. However, the sister ships were both fitted with bow door indicators, watertight bow ramps and freeing flaps to release water from the vehicle decks. International maritime regulations changed in 1990 requiring improved safety features resulting from the lessons learned from the *Herald of Free Enterprise*. The cost of the modifications that had been requested by the senior officers to fit bow door indicators and higher-capacity ballast pumps were of minor value compared to the major cost to people's lives and to the reputation of the company. This is a powerful example of why an organization needs to aspire to be classified as "Pro-Active" (where "management listens to sharp-enders") and "Generative" (where it "strives for resilience"), as described by James Reason in *A Life in Error*.

Mr. Justice Sheen's work in 1987 did a great service to the safe operation of ferries, and the transparency of the report revealed the syndrome of bad management when there is an abdication of the "collective mindfulness." For any system to function—be it a roll-on roll-off ferry, an oil refinery or a steel plan—there must be positive engagement between the individuals at the sharp end and those entrusted with the executive power. When this environment is in harmony, the right culture will be in place. Sadly, for the 193 people who lost their lives on the *Herald of Free Enterprise*, they were victims of a system that failed them.

Six: Estonia, 1994

The *Estonia* was built as the *Viking Sally* and was delivered into service on June 29, 1980, the same year that the Schichau Unterweser shipyard at Bremerhaven delivered the *Herald of Free Enterprise*. The *Viking Sally* was built at the German shipyard of Jos L. Meyer. The *Estonia* was larger than the Spirit class of ferry, being 23.5 meters longer and 1.5 m wider. The service speeds were comparable, at 21 knots on the *Estonia* and 22 knots on the Spirit class. The *Estonia* was fitted with bridge indicator lights to show the position of the bow visor and ramp, which was not the case on the Spirit class.

Notably, the navigating bridge of the *Estonia* was set back from the forward accommodation and this restricted the view such that the bow visor could not be seen by the navigating officers from the bridge when the bow visor was in the closed position. The *Viking Sally* was built for service between Finland and Sweden. This was the regular route until 1993 when the *Viking Sally* was transferred to Estline and refitted for service between the Estonian port of Tallinn and Stockholm in Sweden. According to the formal investigation, on the night of September 28, 1994, the *Estonia* was on her regular voyage to Stockholm having left Tallinn with 989 people onboard.

At about 01:00 the bow visor locking devices failed, and about 15 minutes later the visor fell into the sea, leaving the ramp fully open and exposed to the sea. Within 60 minutes the *Estonia* developed a list to starboard, which continued to increase as the flooding from the open bow increased, until eventually the ferry capsized beneath the waves. The first Mayday call was initiated at 01:22. A brief alarm was given in Estonian over the public address system, but no further information was provided to the passengers. The crew were alerted by the sounding of a fire alarm code. There was no organized evacuation. Only 137 survived.

The final report found the following:
- There were no detailed design requirements for bow visors in the rules of Bureau Veritas, the classification society concerned, at the time of the building of the ESTONIA.
- The Finnish Maritime Administration was, according to a national decree, exempt from doing hull surveys of vessels holding valid class certificates issued by authorized classification societies.
- The visor locking devices were not examined for approval by the Finnish

Maritime Administration, nor by Bureau Veritas.

• The visor design load and the assumed load distribution on the attachments did not take realistic wave impact loads into account.

• The visor locking devices installed were not manufactured in accordance with the design intentions.

• No safety margin was incorporated in the total load carrying capacity of the visor attachment system.

• The attachment system as installed was able to withstand a resultant wave force only slightly above the design load used.

• A long series of bow visor incidents on other ships had not led to general action to reinforce the attachments of bow doors on existing ro-ro passenger ferries, including the ESTONIA.

• Wave impact loads generated on the night of the accident exceeded the combined strength of the visor attachments.

• Wave impact loads on the visor increased very quickly with increasing significant wave height, while forward speed had a smaller effect on the loads.

• The SOLAS requirements for an upper extension of the collision bulkhead were not satisfied.

- The general maintenance standard of the visor was satisfactory. Existing minor maintenance deficiencies were not significant factors in the accident.

Based on the Final Inquiry, the design of the bow visor was not fit for purpose, and the prior bow visor incidents had not resulted in any effort to bring about change. This has resonance with the loss of the *Herald of Free Enterprise* seven years earlier when the Formal Inquiry revealed that prior incidents with the bow doors being left open, the failure to fit remote indicators and other issues had not been actioned. Both of these ferries operated under the pressure of a tight schedule that led to the crews being under pressure. This prioritized productivity over safety, creating a dangerous environment that would allow any latent defect to be activated and moving closer to that final hole in the Swiss Cheese Model.

When I learned about the loss of the *Estonia*, I was visiting a bulk carrier at the port of New Orleans. The surveyor conducting the draught and deadweight survey was Russian a recent immigrant to the United States working as a marine surveyor. During our meeting onboard the subject of the *Estonia* came up, and he explained to me that he was aware that this ferry had known problems with the bow visor. He was adamant that this was the cause of the sinking—this was barely 24 hours after the news had broken on CNN. I do remember he was sure. After all the thorough investigations and underwater surveys, the Final Inquiry confirmed the bow visor had failed. What happened to the *Estonia* highlights one of the most significant challenges to all seafarers: the vulnerability embedded from poor design. The bow visor was a critical component of the *Estonia* in the same way that the bow door closing was on the *Herald of Free Enterprise*. For some reason, the designers of the *Estonia* positioned the navigating bridge set back such that the bow visor could not be seen from the bridge. There are many other cases of design defects that have created problems or latent defects that are built-in to the construction, establishing ongoing challenges for the operating crews.

During my service on Canadian ships, I served as chief officer of a belt-type self-unloading bulk carrier called the *Ontario Power*. The *Ontario Power* was fitted with steam turbine propulsion and steam turbine generators for electrical power. The entire system of propulsion and power onboard was reliant on a single source of high-pressure steam. Steam was supplied by a single water-tube boiler. Most steam-powered ships have multiple boilers to ensure a backup in the event of a blown or leaking tube, an inherent risk in a water-tube boiler.

The *Ontario Power* had been designed and built to service a coal contract from the coal mines and port at Sydney, Nova Scotia to supply coal to a power-generating station in Ontario. This trade required the ship to be built to navigate in the Home Trade waters of Canada. Most of the Canadian Lakes fleet sailed only within the Inland Waters zone and this only permitted them to sail outside the Great Lakes as far as the North shore iron ore ports of Sept Iles and Havre St Pierre in Quebec, all within the Gulf of St Lawrence. Sailing on further to Sydney, Nova Scotia required Home Waters certification, which needed increased scantlings for construction to meet the challenges and rigors of open sea navigation. The Home Waters also included the western and eastern coastlines of Canada, and to connect both Canadian coasts the Home Trade zone included the coastline of the United States and Central America so that Home Trade ships could pass through the Panama Canal. In effect, this provision took these so-called Home Trade ships into some of the most dangerous waters of the Atlantic and the Pacific.

The challenge of a single water-tube boiler was that over time the tubes inside the boiler suffer corrosion on the wall of the tubing, and they become prone to failure. Because the water passes inside the tubes as the hot air heats the tubes to create steam, any leak from a tube has the effect of stopping the production of steam. On the *Ontario Power*, a

110

blown tube was a constant concern, with the prospect of such considered a nightmare, and to make the repair the boiler had to be shut down. The loss of steam meant we lost all main engine propulsion and electrical power. The backup generator, a Caterpillar diesel, would only provide limited emergency power, but we were essentially a "dead ship" hoisting up the twin black ball signal indicating to others that we were "Not Under Command." If this happened during calm sea conditions, we could drift while repairs were being made. When sea conditions were stormy, it was extremely uncomfortable to have the *Ontario Power* laying in the trough of the sea, rolling at the whim of the ocean. Such conditions did not help the efforts of the engineers seeking the identity of the blown tube. The challenge for the chief engineer was that they physically had to gain access inside the boiler to identify the damaged tube and then isolate and seal off that tube. Needless to say, the interior of the boiler was very hot, and the engineers had to wait for the internal temperature to cool down. Once the temperature was tolerable, they would brave the heat and enter to make the repair. The entire process could last several hours, and in the meantime we were at the mercy of the sea. During my time on the *Ontario Power*, we were told that relief was planned in adding an emergency boiler that would provide enough steam for power generation and limited propulsion—enough to at least maintain steering. In the meantime, recognizing the ongoing problem, we were given a second auxiliary diesel generator that came installed inside a 20-foot shipping container. I never saw the emergency boiler fitted and I do not know if this ever happened. The *Ontario Power* went to the breaker's yard ten years after I last sailed on her.

On reflection, I have always wondered why the ship had been designed with a single boiler and how such an arrangement could be considered a smart decision. While it is true that most merchant ships sail around the world powered by a single slow-speed diesel engine, the salient difference is that they have separate diesel generators that provide electrical power, so even if main engine power is down, all the other systems remain on. The reliability of the slow-speed marine diesel engine is also such that downtime is rare unless there is a catastrophic failure of a bearing or major component. In my experience, most problems could be repaired, and they were usually single incidents, not consistent failures like blown tubes. Perhaps the designer thought that the intended route of the *Ontario Power* between Nova Scotia and Ontario was mostly in lakes and rivers and did not foresee a single boiler as a risk. In retrospect, it was a significant defect of the design that was accepted by the owners and the competent authorities.

On the *Estonia*, when the bow visor fell off and the bow was exposed to the sea, the impact of the ship's speed on the rush of water into the open vehicle deck was much the same as the situation on the *Herald of Free Enterprise*, which left the berth in Zeebrugge ballasted down by the head with the bow doors wide open. When Captain Lewry opened up the power of the *Herald*'s massive propulsion capability, the open bow took on water rapidly, and a similar situation occurred on the *Estonia*. The effect for both was a rapidly developing starboard list, and this created a severe change of orientation for all onboard. Transverse passageways became vertical chutes, and the entire system for planned evacuation became a nightmare. Exit routes were blocked and the method to evacuate collapsed because the ship was no longer in the prescribed orientation. This had all been documented in great detail by Justice Sheen at the Formal Inquiry for the *Herald of Free Enterprise* in 1987. The *Estonia* incident took place in 1994. There is an expectation that when a serious loss of life occurs, the primary purpose of the investigation is to understand the root cause so that lessons can be learned and applied in order to prevent a repeat occurrence. What we know is 852 people's lives were cut short because the latent defect present in the bow visor was not the subject of sufficient dialog to effect change. In addition, the findings of the *Herald of Free Enterprise* report had covered the grave difficulty of passenger evacuation on ferries with extreme angles of list, and the same circumstances hampered those trying to escape the *Estonia*.

Another example of the effect of awareness and how different organizations engage in dialog that sets them on different paths is the story of three Shell Tankers VLCC's. In December 1969, three Shell Tankers, the *Mactra*, *Marpessa*, and the *Kong Haakon VII* all suffered massive explosions while in ballast and tank cleaning. The Dutch flag *Marpessa* sank off Dakar, the British flag *Mactra* and the Norwegian flag *King Haakon VII* were heavily damaged but remained afloat.

In 1969, there was no regulatory requirement to fit inert gas systems on tankers. Such systems existed and were in use by other owners, notably BP Shipping. BP had been troubled by excessive corrosion in their tankers carrying crude oil, and they realized the installation and use of an onboard inert gas system would substantially reduce the loss of steel. BP recognized that the cost of installing and operating an inert gas system was far less than the cost of replacing steel or a reduced active life for their tankers.

Following the three explosions, Shell conducted research and discovered that, during tank cleaning, the large tanks on a VLCC were prone to creating static electricity as the jets of water rotated around the tanks. Tanks were washed by patented washing machines with jets of pressurized seawater. The jets rotated using a gearing system that causes them to turn in all directions, to ensure that the jets would pass over every part of the interior of the tank. This method of tank cleaning had been standard operating practice on smaller tankers, and the naval architects had merely scaled up to meet the needs of the much larger tanks on a VLCC. However, nobody had carried out any tests or considered the implications of what would happen inside a huge enclosed tank. The atmosphere inside the tank was highly volatile because the tank contained residual crude oil vapors and large amounts of oxygen. Therefore, any spark from any source would cause a massive explosion. This is what happened to the *Mactra* and the *Kong Haakon VII*, and most likely the *Marpessa*.

Following the three incidents, Shell rapidly altered course and introduced inert gas systems to its entire fleet. Legislation would follow behind, and this illustrates an important point about vulnerability emanating from ship design. The reality of rules and regulations is that they are reactive to events: change comes after something goes wrong. This was the case for the introduction of load lines and the tireless campaign of Samuel Plimsoll. Plimsoll realized that the so-called "Coffin ships" carrying coal to provide fuel for nineteenth-century London were capsizing and being lost with terrible frequency, giving rise to seafarers calling the coal ships "Coffin ships."

The shipping industry was against the imposition of rules that would govern the maximum amount of cargo they could carry. Fortunately, Samuel Plimsoll prevailed, and consequently, every ship around the world bears witness to his campaign by displaying the white circle with a line through the center known as the Plimsoll mark.

In 1912 the loss of the *Titanic* would see the introduction of legislation regarding the carriage of lifeboat capacity for all crew and passengers. The loss of the *Derbyshire* and many other large bulk carriers led to changes in the rules for hatch cover strength. The *Marine Electric* led to the US Coast Guard diver/swimmer rescue program and immersion suits for seafarers. The *Herald of Free Enterprise* led to changes in roll-on, roll-off ferry regulations. The *Exxon Valdez* led to the Oil Pollution Act 1990 in the United States, which mandated the introduction of double-hulled tankers. There are many more examples that can be cited— what we can observe is that change evolves through interference, and the catalyst frequently requires energy from a loss of life or loss of property or both.

This phenomenon is not unique to the shipping industry. The Grenfell fire in London has resulted in an inquiry that will most likely lead to change in construction and building material regulations, plus fire and rescue procedures. Therefore, anyone who is engaged in any aspect of operating any system where Process Safety applies needs to have an awareness of their environment. At the sharp end of any process, there will be latent defects waiting to surprise. Learning how to recognize their existence requires dialog with others to ascertain the risks. Risk management in my view is the ability to see around the corner to visualize what is yet to happen. There are various safety programs championed by Esso, DuPont and others all advising workers to take the time to think and dialog before taking action—these are all designed to create a pause to think before acting.

A good example of an incident where the application of risk management could have prevented a major loss was the grounding of the tanker *Braer* off the Shetland Islands in Scotland in January 1993.

The *Braer* was caught in a severe storm on her loaded voyage from Norway to Canada. The *Braer* had some steel pipes stored on the weather deck near the accommodation intended for use in future repair work. During the storm, the *Braer* was rolling heavily, and the pipes broke loose. The master failed to recognize the risk and did not make any attempt to re-secure the pipes. The loose pipes damaged the air ventilation pipes to the ship's fuel tanks. This led to a cascade of events as the *Braer* made her way through successive holes in the Swiss Cheese Model. Seawater contaminated the fuel and led to the shutdown of the auxiliary boiler. This, in turn, made it impossible to heat the heavy fuel oil to achieve the right viscosity. The engineers then switched over to diesel fuel for the main engine and the auxiliary generators. They shut down when the diesel fuel became contaminated. The *Braer* was now a dead ship drifting in a major storm towards the rocks. Despite valiant attempts to dispatch powerful tugs to prevent the *Braer* from grounding, all attempts failed. However, all the crew were rescued by Coast Guard helicopters. The master and the officers of the *Braer* did not "look around the corner" to consider the location of the steel pipes and what would happen if they were to break free of their securing. They missed a latent defect and were unable to comprehend the consequence even after the pipes had first broken loose. Consequently, 85,000 tons of crude oil was spilled into the sea and the ship was a total loss.

On the *Estonia,* there is a possibility that had the risk of the bow visor been fully understood they may have adopted a procedure to manage the risk by reducing speed during sea conditions where the bow visor would have been exposed to excessive force. The reduced sailing speed would mean a longer voyage and a more flexible schedule. Compare this to the general acceptance when it comes to air travel. When the pilot of a commercial airliner advises that turbulence is affecting the plane, they change course and deviate to avoid the problem. If that means arriving late, is that a problem? When weather conditions at airports require de-icing procedures, flights are delayed because this takes time and planes can only be de-iced just before takeoff. All these are considered an acceptable inconvenience. Therefore, if a marine ferry must slow down to weather conditions why should that be any different?

In some cases, the simple malfunction of a component in the machinery can lead to a rolling, steadily exacerbating chain of events. In the summer of 1976, I was standing my evening 4–8 watch onboard the *Phosphore Conveyor*, a Panamax bulk carrier. We were heading north off the Virginia coast near Cape Hatteras heading to Canada with a full cargo of phosphate rock. Weather and sea conditions were good. Shortly after nautical twilight, I observed a white light dead ahead at close range. I feared that we had come upon a yachtsman and that they had switched on their running light as they saw our shape and lights bearing down upon them. I had little time to react: we were making 15 knots with the Gulf stream current in our favor. Our 106-foot beam and deadweight made us a formidable force for any small yacht. I immediately took the ship out of autopilot and put the helm hard over to starboard to miss whatever was shining a light. As we did that, I had my lookout go to the port bridge wing to see what was out there. Having executed the emergency turn, I then put the helm to midships to resume our course. However, to my shock, the rudder remained hard to starboard, and we were now going in a circle at full speed. I notified the master and called the engine room and brought the main engines to stop. As we continued to circle our pace slowed as the way came off. Our hydraulic steering gear had failed and locked in the full starboard position.

The engineers spent the next two hours working on the problem in the steering gear room, while we sat motionless in the Atlantic with two red "not under command" lights on display. They discovered that a rubber "O" ring had failed in the control system, causing the steering gear to become locked. Repairs were made, and we realized the entire affair had revealed a latent defect that could have caused much greater trouble had this taken place during our frequent trips up and down the Orinoco River. The Orinoco has many tight turns, and they can only be made at full speed and full rudder. Had our steering gear failed us in the Orinoco we would have been hard aground in the Venezuelan jungle. We never did identify the source of the white light that led to the emergency turn. In retrospect, I have always considered the white light to be a gift.

The *Phosphore Conveyor* was not the only large ship to suffer a steering gear failure. Two years later, in March 1978, the VLCC tanker *Amoco Cadiz* was fully loaded, having just passed Ushant off the Brittany coast of France. The *Amoco Cadiz* had made a course change to avoid another ship and her rudder jammed hard to port. Repairs were not successful, and the Northwesterly winds caused the *Amoco Cadiz* to drift towards the Portsall rocks. Salvage attempts failed, and the *Amoco Cadiz* broke up on the rocks, disgorging 220,000 tons of crude oil into the sea. The story of the failed rubber "O" ring on the steering gear of the *Phosphore Conveyor* is reminiscent of the proverb, "For want of a nail the kingdom was lost." There are many versions, but the one most familiar to me is that which speaks of King Richard III at the battle of Bosworth Field in 1485. In 1986, when the *Challenger* space shuttle orbiter broke apart at the launch, killing all seven astronauts, it was the failure of an "O" ring seal that was the ultimate cause. I have always had great respect for the humble "O" ring. For want of an "O" ring, the steering was lost.

Estline had been a joint venture between the Swedish company Nordstrom and Thulin and the Estonian government. Four years after the loss of the *Estonia*, Nordstrom and Thulin left the joint venture. Estline went bankrupt in 2001. Today two ferry services operate on the route followed by the *Estonia*, the Tallink Silja service and St Peter Line, Notably, the new ferries are wider, allowing for turning within the vehicle deck, thereby eliminating the need for bow doors.

The loss of the *Estonia* is a reminder of vulnerability and the management of risk. There were issues with the design and build of the *Estonia*. These could have been mitigated by adopting an operating plan that embraced the risk instead of ignoring it. It is wise to realize that there is a potential for failure in systems that have yet to fail. This is what happened to the three Shell VLCCs that exploded during tank cleaning. They met all the regulations required of them, but there was no awareness of the risk of creating static electricity inside the tanks while washing. BP had taken a different course to fit an inert gas system, but their reason was to mitigate another concern, corrosion. Vulnerability is also about situational awareness—the ability to look around the corner and to see a future risk. On the *Braer*, had the master and chief officer given more thought to the stowage and securing of the steel pipe, they would not have ended up as a permanent fixture in the Shetlands. For the *Braer*, "For want of individual mindfulness—the *Braer* and her cargo were lost into the ocean." Then there are the small unseen components like the rubber "O" ring that bring failure. In the case of the *Estonia,* their "O" ring was the poorly designed bow visor. The wreck of the *Estonia* remains resting on the bed of the Baltic Sea.

Seven: Sewol, 2014

On the morning of April 16, 2014, the South Korean ferry *Sewol* was completing her regular southbound run from Incheon to Jeju. That morning the *Sewol* had a crew of 33 with 443 passengers onboard. Among the passengers were 325 high school students from Danwon High School taking a field trip to Jeju Island accompanied by their teachers. The *Sewol* entered service on March 15, 2013, making a regular run between Incheon and Jeju Island. Three round trips were made each week, and the one-way voyage typically lasted 13.5 hours. The *Sewol* had departed Incheon later than planned on April 15, due to dense fog at the port of Incheon, leaving at 9 pm instead of 6:30 pm as scheduled. The weather on the morning of April 16 was calm, the *Sewol* was on a course of 165 degrees at a speed of 20 knots. At 08:20 the third officer switched from auto-pilot to manual steering in preparation for the course changes required to navigate the Maenggol Channel. At 08:46 the third officer instructed the helmsman to change course to starboard, and at 08:48 a further starboard course change was given. At 08:49 the *Sewol* suddenly listed to port by 20 degrees, and this led to cargo breaking free and shifting to the port side. The shift of cargo exacerbated the list to port. The chief engineer stopped the engines and ordered an evacuation of the engine room. The first emergency call was received at 08:52 from one of the Danwon High School students, Choi Duk-ha, who used his mobile phone to call the National Emergency number. Choi could not provide the emergency services with any information about the position of the *Sewol*, he just believed something was wrong. Despite being the first to raise the alarm, Choi was unable to evacuate and did not survive. The first distress call from the *Sewol* was made at 08:55 to the Jeju vessel traffic service. That call was then relayed to the Korean Coast Guard. By 09:14 the *Sewol* was listed to port by 50 degrees and slowly capsizing as water entered her hull through submerged doors and openings.

Onboard the *Sewol,* the engineers had evacuated the engine room, the captain and crew had assembled on the bridge, but remarkably the passengers had been instructed to remain in their cabins, and this order was never changed. At 09:30, with rescue vessels and Coast Guard attending, the captain made the decision to evacuate and abandon ship. By about 9:41 am an estimated 160 crew and passengers jumped overboard and were rescued. However, the rest of the passengers, mostly students who had obeyed the orders to remain in their cabins, never received any instructions to abandon ship. By 11:18 the *Sewol* was almost submerged and at 12:00

only the bulbous bow was visible. By 1:03 pm the *Sewol* disappeared along with 304 people, most of them the high school students from Danwon.

Memorial Bell presented to the Philadelphia SESAMO group by David Reid
April 16, 2017

In the summer of 1967, I went on my own school cruise on board the British India Steam Navigation school ship *Nevasa*. The *Nevasa* had been built as a troopship in 1955 and served in that capacity carrying British troops during the Suez Crisis. Ships' role in moving troops became redundant with the availability of commercial aircraft in the early sixties. The *Nevasa* was laid up for several years, and in 1965, British India converted the *Nevasa* to operate as an educational cruise ship. As a school ship, *Nevasa* was configured to house students in dormitory style accommodation below decks, and approximately 1,000 children could be carried. Our cruise was a two-week trip in July 1967 from the Port of London to Scandinavia and on to the Baltic port of Leningrad in the Soviet Union. There were about a hundred of us from my school in the northwest suburbs of London.

Pinner County Grammar — 1967 School Cruise departing for the *Nevasa* cruise; by permission of Pinner Old Students Association.

Leaving London, we had our first lifeboat drill. We put on our lifejackets and proceeded to the boat deck where we mustered underneath the white lifeboat nestled in its davits above us. We stood quietly in rows as a head count was made. I do not remember any guidance being given about how we would embark into the lifeboats. The main activity that day seemed to be a ship's version of school assembly, except in a lifejacket.

We headed to Norway for our first port call and then on to the Swedish Island of Visby in the Baltic. Onboard we had a strict schedule of activities. Lights in the dormitory came on at 6 am, and the quartermaster gave us our wake-up call. At the end of each day, we were in our dormitory, and the lights went off by 9:30 pm. The dorms onboard the *Nevasa* were segregated by gender, with the boys forward of the engine room and the girls towards the stern. At all times the dormitories were always under strict surveillance by the quartermasters and matrons. Due to the large number on board, we had to be in the cafeteria at our allotted time slot, so this meant our quartermaster constantly reminded us of the need to hurry along. During the day we had educational classes onboard because we were technically still in school. However, we did get some free time to spend on deck, and this was the only time we were allowed to spend mixing with the girls. Our cruise also had about 500 Canadian students, of a similar age to us. This was the summer of 1967, and the Beatles had just released their new album *Sgt. Pepper's Lonely-Hearts Club Band.*

It also meant we arrived in Leningrad (St Petersburg) in the summer of the fiftieth anniversary of the 1917 Bolshevik Revolution. We would be in the port of Leningrad for the most extended port call of the entire cruise. The first day in Leningrad we all went ashore in our respective school groups with our teachers acting as our shepherds. We then boarded coaches and were taken on a guided tour of the city with frequent stops to get off and walk around a church or a museum.

In the evening, those of us whose parents had paid the extra fee for us to go on by train to Moscow left for the railway station to board the overnight sleeper train. A special train had been organized just for the cruise ship students. We were in good spirits as we left Leningrad station, with our heads out of the windows singing our version of "Rule Britannia"!

Moscow was fascinating. We visited Red Square. We filed past Vladimir Lenin and paid our respects. As tourists, we were allowed to go to the front of the long line patiently waiting to enter Lenin's mausoleum. On both days we had been changing money into rubles, the local currency, and we were excited because we were receiving far more rubles than the 'official' exchange rate. When we learned that we could have some time to spend our money in the tourist shop, we were expecting to reap great dividends of spending power, until we discovered the tourist shop only accepted payment in foreign currency—not rubles. That evening we went to the Bolshoi Theatre to see the ballet. I had never been in such a grand building, and this was my first experience of the ballet. At 16, I was supposed to consider ballet somewhat silly, but the more I watched and listened, the more I began to appreciate the music and the beauty of the dancing. On our voyage back to London our final port call was Copenhagen in Denmark, and a visit to the Tivoli gardens.

The cruise on the *Nevasa* was my first travel outside of England, and I know that I came home a different person with my eyes opened to the world. I was soon to be 17. I was the same age as many of the Danwon High School students, who were no doubt excited to be on a ship overnight with their school friends to spend time on Jeju Island, a favorite holiday destination for Koreans.

The Danwon High School students were instructed to remain in their cabins, and their obedience to authority is embedded in the Neo-Confucian culture. Following the *Sewol* disaster an article in the *Singapore Times* made the following observation: "Like other Asian nations, South Korean society is based on a Neo-Confucian culture which emphasizes obedience to authority figures and deference to elders. In the wake of the *Sewol* sinking, these values are being called into question." Thinking back to my own experience in 1967 as a teenager on a school ship—if we had been instructed to remain in our dormitory, we would probably have acted in the same way that the Danwon students did on the *Sewol*. I remember how difficult it was to navigate our way within the labyrinth of alleyways and stairs from the dormitories, which were in the bowels of the ship, to reach the upper decks. The lower you are inside a ship, the less effect you feel when the ship has a list. The Danwon High School students were not experienced mariners, they would not have had any means to understand why or what was going on. They would have accepted and relied on their elders to provide instruction.

By the time the cabins began to flood, with the *Sewol* then having a severe list, the interior of the *Sewol* would have been pitch black. The Danwon students had only been onboard the ship for 12 hours, and the chaos and confusion, and the extreme difficulty of finding their way around the inside of a ship now laying on its side would have been extremely challenging. We know from both the *Herald of Free Enterprise* and the *Estonia* that when ferries capsize with severe lists, the interior passageways and exit routes are a serious problem for evacuation. Looking back on my cruise onboard the *Nevasa*, I cannot say that we would have acted any differently to the Danwon students.

Why did the *Sewol* take a sudden list to port during the starboard turn in the Maenggol Channel?

The *Sewol* had been built in Japan and had served 18 years, operating successfully as the *Ferry Naminoue* owned by A-Line. In October 2012, Korean owners Chonghaejin Marine acquired the *Sewol* and undertook a series of modifications. The modifications resulted in significant changes to the transverse stability of the *Sewol*. The owners added additional passenger capacity, seeking to increase revenue. The Korean Register of Shipping offset the higher structure by reducing the amount of cargo that could be carried by 1,450 tons and increasing the amount of ballast by 1,333 tons. The extra ballast was to be carried in double bottom tanks to provide additional stability below the ship's center of gravity. The reduction of cargo carried in the upper decks would reduce the weights above the center of gravity. The combined effect would be to counterbalance the structural changes, thereby giving the *Sewol* a positive GM or metacentric height. The metacentric height is a mathematical measure of the restoring force that keeps a ship upright. However, the *Sewol* left Incheon in direct violation of her stability loading manual, with less ballast—only 761 tons—and much more cargo, at 2,143 tons.

The ship was not loaded deeper than her Plimsoll mark, but the loading was unsafe because the *Sewol* was unstable. The chief officer had purposely pumped out the ballast tanks to offset the additional cargo onboard. The only way he could prevent the *Sewol's* Plimsoll mark from being submerged was to remove the ballast, which was critical to ensuring adequate transverse stability.

When a ship is unstable, it is known to be in a "tender" condition, and that means the ship has reduced or limited capability or restoring force to return upright. In effect, the ship is so finely balanced the strength of a helm order can cause the ship to list and result in what is known as an angle of loll. The captain knew of the stability problem, and so did the chief officer. The captain had of course advised the third officer to be careful when making changes because the *Sewol* had a low restoring force. This latent defect of improper loading resulted in insufficient stability and was the primary cause of the *Sewol* capsizing. The shifting of the cargo during the initial list to port, due to improper lashing and securing, was the second defect, and this caused the ship to list further and flood her compartments, and ultimately to sink.

In the case of all the ships in previous chapters, the incidents all took place at night and quickly, in most cases during extreme weather conditions. The *Sewol* capsize took place in broad daylight and in good weather. There was time to rescue everyone— rescue support was on the scene very quickly. Had the order been given for all passengers to proceed to their muster stations there is a strong possibility that all or nearly all would have been rescued. The chief engineer wasted no time instructing his engineers to evacuate the engine room, and the captain and crew were the first to be rescued. There was an absolute breakdown of communication concerning the care and custody of the passengers. In the period from 9 am to 11 am the passengers trapped inside the *Sewol* were ignored or forgotten by the captain and the rescuers. In an interview with six teenage students that survived, the *Independent* newspaper reported on July 28, 2014, that the girls said: "The door was above our heads, so she said we'll float and go through the door, and that's how we came out. Other children who got out before us pulled us out." The article went on to note, "The teenagers were critical of coastguard officers, who allegedly waited on boats at a distance from the stricken ferry for passengers to swim out rather than going into the ship to try and rescue them."

The hearts of the Korean people were full of pain for the loss of so many young students. A campaign for truth began under the SESAMO ("People in Solidarity with the Families of the *Sewol* Ferry") banner, with concerned groups of Korean nationals around the world coming together to support it via the website 416family.org. The Philadelphia SESAMO group approached the Seamen's Church

Institute ("SCI") of Philadelphia and South Jersey to discuss a memorial service on the third anniversary of the disaster. One of their members had attended a Christmas service for seafarers at the SCI chapel and inquired if the chapel could be used for the memorial service. As one of the port chaplains, I offered to put together a remembrance service, and explained to the group I had my own connection to South Korea through my adopted daughter, who was born in Seoul and had been an orphan before arriving in the United States at the age of four.

Through my daughter's life, I had many experiences of Korean culture and had traveled to Korea many times, including my first visit to the port of Incheon in 1969. My grandchildren were just starting high school, and I considered the opportunity to assist the Philadelphia Korean-American community a privilege.

Several planning meetings took place, and I gave much thought to how we could use the time to honor the 304 lives lost while simultaneously restoring hope for truth and bringing about change to ensure that lessons had been learned. April 16, 2017, also happened to be Easter Sunday in the Christian calendar. To accommodate every persons schedule the *Sewol* service was planned for the late afternoon with a fellowship reception to follow. The chapel was adorned with 304 yellow ribbons, each bearing the name of a person lost. I arranged for a brass ship's bell to be made and engraved with the name of the *Sewol* and the digits "304." We placed that on the altar table draped with a yellow cloth. At the opening of the service, I asked the oldest and youngest person to come forward to ring the bell. The oldest lady rang the bell three times, and then we had a moment of silence, and the youngest lady rang the bell four times. This was a special moment of reflection and prayer to remember the 304 lost. Later in the service, everyone came forward to the altar and the bell to light a candle, so that they could individually have a moment of meditation.

April 16, 2017, — Memorial Service at the SCI Chapel in Philadelphia; by permission of the Seamen's Church Institute of Philadelphia and South Jersey.

One by one, everyone came forward and lit a candle. As they did, the atmosphere in the chapel was full of compassion for each of those yellow ribbons on either side of the chapel. The memorial service for the *Sewol* has been the most significant moment of my work as a chaplain. As a seafarer and former navigator. I also understand the failings of the captain and crew. I know that they were under stress, operating within a system flawed by the actions the owners of the *Sewol* had engineered. I also recognize the dilemma of complacency that had descended over the *Sewol*. With each week of operation, three more round trips were accomplished, making voices of concern and resistance dissipate because nobody was listening. Like so many repetitive actions, they fell into an acceptance of near-misses as part of their normal routine.

When I met and came to know the leaders of the Philadelphia SESAMO group, I was struck by their heartfelt compassion and interest in this maritime disaster. Shortly after the memorial service, the news of another maritime disaster involving Korean seafarers came to the attention of the Philadelphia SESAMO group. This time it was the sinking of the Very Large Ore Carrier, *Stellar Daisy* in the South Atlantic, a ship that will be covered in Chapter Nine. The *Stellar Daisy* was sailing under the Marshall Islands flag but was beneficially owned by a Korean company, and the majority of the crew were South Korean. The Philadelphia SESAMO group reached out to me, asking many questions about the *Stellar Daisy*, and we had a lengthy dialog as I did my best to explain the workings of the world of shipping. They found it difficult to comprehend why a South Korean owned ship was under the flag of a tiny island in the South Pacific.

In my advice to the Philadelphia SESAMO group, I explained to them the story of the British Ore carrier *Derbyshire* (Chapter Three) and the tireless campaign mounted by the families of the seafarers who lost their lives when the *Derbyshire* sank off Japan in 1980. I told them that the Derbyshire Families Association had used their voices to mount a 20-year campaign that resulted in a new inquiry leading to new findings about the loss of the *Derbyshire*. That, in turn, led to improvements in ship design that came to benefit many. They asked me for advice on what the Korean families could do concerning the lost Korean seafarers on the *Stellar Daisy*, and my suggestion was to follow the same path followed by the *Derbyshire* families.

The initial response from the South Korean government was to resist any calls to salvage the *Sewol*. The Korean Coast Guard was disbanded following its failure to conduct a proper search and rescue operation. The captain, chief officer, second officer, and chief engineer were indicted on charges of homicide through gross negligence, and another 11 crew members faced other charges.

On November 11, 2014, the Gwangju District court found Captain Lee Jun-seok guilty and sentenced him to 36 years in prison. The chief engineer received a sentence of 30 years, and 13 other crew members received lesser sentences. On appeal, Captain Lee Jun-seok's sentence was increased to life imprisonment, and the chief engineer was reduced to ten years. The CEO of Chonghaejin Marine was initially sentenced to a 10-year term, reduced to 7 years after an appeal. Six other management employees were convicted together with an employee of the Korean Shipping Association.

Following the capsizing of the *Sewol*, in May 2014, the owners Chonghaejin Marine were stripped of their license to operate ferries by the South Korean Ministry of Oceans and Fisheries. In June 2014 the company went into receivership. On June 12, 2014, Yoo Byung-eun, the chairman of Chonghaejin Marine, was found dead in a field.

On April 27, 11 days after the *Sewol* capsized, the prime minister of South Korea, Jung Hon-Won resigned his position and accepted responsibility for the *Sewol*. Two days later the president Park Geun-

Hye apologized for the government's response to the sinking of the *Sewol*. One month after the loss the president announced the Korean Coast Guard would be disbanded. This became effective on November 19, 2014, with a new Ministry of Public Safety and Security taking its place.

On April 17, Chonghaejin Marine the owners of the *Sewol* made an apology. On April 28, 2014, the chairman and CEO of the Korean Register of Shipping resigned following investigative raids on the offices of the Korean Register by Korean prosecutors.

On a somber and reflective note, on April 18 Kang Min-kyu, the vice principal of Danwon High School, took his own life. Kang had planned the field trip for his students and had himself been rescued. The note found in his wallet read: "Surviving alone is too painful when 200 lives are unaccounted for... I take full responsibility." Kang's note requested his body be cremated and his ashes scattered over the sea at the site of the wreck, in order, as Kang wrote, "That I might be a teacher in heaven to those kids whose bodies have not been found."

The people of South Korea began a peaceful campaign with the symbol of the yellow ribbon and the mantra to never forget 4/16/19, the date that 304 lost their lives. Candlelight vigils brought thousands of Koreans together expressing their demands for truth and justice. The president of South Korea at the time, Park Geun-Hye, was already involved in a political corruption scandal, and the *Sewol* tragedy and the failure of the administration became a focal point for the impeachment of the president. The candlelight vigils in Gwanghwamun Square in Seoul began on October 26, 2016 and resulted in more than one million people assembling to express their emotions. The candlelight vigils continued weekly until the South Korean president had been removed from office on March 10, 2017. On May 5, 2017, the new South Korean president Moon Jae-in was sworn in.

The task of salvaging the wreck of the *Sewol* was put out to bid to salvage companies. On July 15, 2015, the winning bid was awarded to the Chinese Shanghai Salvage Company. The value of the proposal was 74.6 million dollars. On March 22, 2017, the salvage operation began. The *Sewol* was lying on her port side at a depth of 40 meters. The operation was hampered by the strong currents and prevailing weather conditions. The salvage operation consisted of three phases:

Phase One: Raising the *Sewol* to the surface using two crane barges.

Phase Two: Loading the *Sewol* on to a semi-submersible ship and then carrying the *Sewol* to the port of Mokpo.

Phase Three: Transferring the *Sewol* ashore and returning her to an upright position.

On March 31, 2017, the semi-submersible ship *Dockwise White Marlin* brought the *Sewol* to the port of Mokpo. At Mokpo the stricken hull of the *Sewol* was gently transferred to land using a large assembly of self-propelled hydraulic transporters that carried the hull from the deck of the *Dockwise White Marlin* to rest on stands set up within the shipyard. The final move used an "L" shape set of beams placed under the port side of the hull and against her bottom plating, forming a cradle. They employed two large floating cranes attached to both sides of the cradle, and the cradle was rotated about its fulcrum point by 90 degrees to bring the *Sewol* upright.

The entire cost of the salvage operation was borne by the government of South Korea, and is notable for the complexity of the operation and the significance to the people of South Korea. The interior of the *Sewol* has been forensically surveyed in the hopes of finding the final missing persons. The five whose bodies were never found were given their funeral service on November 20, 2017. Of the five, two were boys, students from Danwon High School, and one was a teacher from the high school. The remaining two were father and son Kwon Jae-geun and six-year-old Kwon Hyeok-gyu. The Kwon family was moving to Jeju Island, and the mother Han Yun-ji also died. Only their youngest daughter Kwon Ji-yeon survived. Reports said that six-year-old Hyeok-gyu had helped his little sister escape by putting on her lifejacket. This simple act by a six-year-old-boy amid the chaos and confusion stands out as one of those special moments that symbolize compassionate acts to help others. Clearly, Hyeok-gyu had no training in emergency procedures, so what he did was a perfect display of humanity at its finest.

When I read about this story in the Hankyoreh newspaper, I recognized the actions of Hyeok-gyu to be a reminder of the selfless acts of compassion displayed by the story of the four chaplains onboard the SS *Dorchester* in 1943. The *Dorchester* was a US Army troop ship on its way to a base in Greenland. During the night of February 3, 1943, the *Dorchester* was struck by a torpedo from a German submarine. The effect was immediate: the *Dorchester* sank rapidly, and the abandon ship order was given. The soldiers had been instructed to sleep with their lifejackets on. However, many did not follow these instructions and in a rush to abandon ship they were in desperate need of lifejackets. On board the *Dorchester* that night there were four army chaplains. These four chaplains took up positions on the deck, handing out lifejackets to the soldiers who were jumping into the cold waters of the Atlantic Ocean. Fortunately, two Coast Guard cutters were close by, and they were busy picking up survivors before they succumbed to hypothermia.

When the supply of spare lifejackets ran out, the four chaplains took off their jackets and handed them to the young soldiers. Each chaplain was of a different faith group, but on that night, they acted to save everyone, and they did so with uniformity. The survivors said that the last they saw of the four chaplains was them holding each other and singing as they went down with the ship. The story of those four chaplains—Lt. George L. Fox (Methodist), Lt. Alexander D. Goode (Judaic), Lt. John P. Washington (Catholic), and Lt. Clark V. Poling (Dutch Reformed)—is carried on today through the Four Chaplains Memorial Foundation based at the Navy Yard in Philadelphia. The mission statement is simply "Unity Without Uniformity." Yearly, they recognize individuals around the world "[w]hose lives model the giving spirit and unconditional service to community, nation, and humanity without regard to race, religion, or creed exemplified so dramatically by the Four Chaplains." The actions of six-year-old Hyeok-gyu on that morning of April 16, 2014, remind us that in the midst of great adversity there are incredible acts of compassion and love.

The story of the *Sewol* galvanized the people of South Korea to attain a level of awareness about their domestic maritime industry, and once their consciousness had been raised, they maintained the pressure to bring about change. The campaign went on far beyond the Danwon High School and Seoul the capital city. The tragedy of the *Sewol* contributed to the impeachment of the president and the disbanding of the Korean Coast Guard. These are events that have never happened in any other nation following a maritime tragedy.

For the people of South Korea, the truth is the *Sewol* did not have to capsize off Jindo Island on that morning in April. The pathogens—the latent defects—were introduced into the system when the ferry was purchased from Japan and converted. The conversion introduced serious stability defects, which became patently obvious to the operators. When they raised their concerns, the management refused to listen. The commercial pressure applied by the management to load more cargo while carrying less compensating ballast applied a systemic and powerful force to those onboard the *Sewol*. They could have refused to sail and given up their employment, knowing that someone else would fill their slot. Perhaps they rationalized that they would do better to remain with the *Sewol* because they understood the risks and as long as they were careful, it could be managed. This is the disease of complacency, and each week as three more round voyages were made, they continued their skate on thin ice. Complacency creates a false sense of confidence, reminiscent of other incidents where prudent action is forgotten and replaced by an attitude of foolish invincibility. On first inspection, it would be easy to place the root cause with the captain and the chief officer, but the real issue rests with the systemic failure of the owners and management. The systemic failure echoed the words of Justice Sheen during the Formal Inquiry into the loss of the *Herald of Free Enterprise* when he stated: "From top to bottom the body corporate was infected with the disease of sloppiness." In the case of South Korea, the Korean people were to find that the disease of sloppiness had infected their entire maritime structure, from the highest levels in government and down through layers of authority. The Danwon High School students on the *Sewol* will not be forgotten by the nation of South Korea; they will serve as a constant reminder to future generations that this can never happen again.

Eight: El Faro, 2015

October 1, 2015, marks the day that the United States Merchant Marine suffered the loss of the *El Faro* with all hands. The *El Faro* was built in 1975 at the former Sun shipyard on the Delaware River just south of Philadelphia. *El Faro* means "the lighthouse" in Spanish, and the ship operated on a shuttle service between Jacksonville, Florida and San Juan, Puerto Rico. This route is considered a US domestic route and is therefore governed by the provisions of the Jones Act, which stipulates that only ships owned by US Citizens, built in US shipyards and manned by US Citizens and/or permanent residents can operate on these routes. The Jones Act is section 27 of the Merchant Marine Act of 1920. The act was introduced by Senator Wesley Jones and specifically covers the coastwise trade, also known as cabotage. Cabotage is defined as trade carried out within the restriction of a particular territory or country. The United States is not alone in the application of laws relating to cabotage—China, South Korea, Russia, Japan, Chile, Mexico, Brazil, Argentina, Australia, Canada, and many others also have laws pertaining to it.

The intention of the United States Congress in passing such laws was to ensure a vibrant United States maritime industry and for reasons of national defense. In reality, over the period of almost 100 years, the United States maritime industry has declined. The Maritime Administration of the US Department of Transport (MARAD) reported in January 2018 that only 100 privately owned oceangoing self-propelled vessels are engaged in domestic trade, with only 82 engaged in international trade. Notably, they also report that the US flag share of foreign trade is only 1.54%. The story of the *El Faro* and what happened on October 1, 2015, is embedded into the skirts of cabotage.

El Faro was owned and operated by the TOTE group, a subsidiary of the Saltchuk company. In 1985 they created Sea Star Line and began operating the Puerto Rico service using three sister ships the *El Faro*, *El Yunque* and *El Morro* between Jacksonville and San Juan, Puerto Rico. The *El Morro* was withdrawn from service and scrapped in 2014. In September 2015, shortly before the loss of the *El Faro*, Sea Star Line changed their name to TOTE Maritime Puerto Rico. TOTE had two new ships under construction in San Diego to replace the aging *El Faro* and *El Yunque*. The new constructions, known as the Marlin class, would be pure container vessels with no roll-on, roll-off capability. TOTE planned to convert the *El Faro* back to pure roll-on roll-off and to deploy her in the Alaska run to provide cover while their two Alaska trailer-ships, *Midnight Sun* (built in 2003) and *North Star* (built in 2003), were undergoing conversions to become dual-fueled.

El Faro left Jacksonville fully loaded with trailers, cars, and containers. The latent defects were identified in the Marine Board of Inquiry report. The *El Faro* encountered the effects of Hurricane Joaquim. She had minimal freeboard and due to the deck loading of containers, her transverse stability was reduced and as a result the *El Faro* heeled to starboard due to the sustained winds. The *El Faro* had ventilation scuttles on each side that were compromised due to corrosion, were not watertight and were routinely left open. The list allowed seawater ingress, and this exacerbated the starboard list. Cargo securing failed as a result of the list, and this further exacerbated the list. The master attempted to correct the starboard list by pumping ballast and turning the ship against the wind. This resulted in a port list that was greater than the starboard list. The severe port list caused a loss of propulsion when the steam turbines lost suction to the lubricating oil in the sump. The *El Faro* then fell into the trough of the sea and rapidly began flooding through various openings, sinking before any attempt to abandon ship could be made. The *El Faro* sank to the seabed and rests 15,300 feet below the surface. All 33 persons are missing and presumed deceased.

Thirty-two years before the *El Faro* capsized, carrying her entire crew and cargo to the seabed, another Jones Act ship, the *Marine Electric*, had met a similar fate off the Virginia coast. The respective inquiries into the circumstances that led to the loss of the *Marine Electric* and the *El Faro* found extensive commonalities and raise serious questions about the process of those who are charged to regulate and oversee an industry that operates under the protection of cabotage. A student of Charles Perrow, the author of *Normal Accidents*, wrote his Ph.D. thesis in 1990 at the State University of New York. The title of Leo Lawrence Tasca's thesis was "The Social Construction of Human Error." Tasca focused his research on the analysis of four maritime incidents. His findings reveal flaws in the system of maritime accident investigation and the ability to learn lessons from them. Tasca wrote the following with respect to the age of ships:

> "The *Poet* and the *Marine Electric* were, respectively, thirty-five and thirty-eight years old. The media and maritime unions offered considerable 'evidence' designed to link the accidents with vessel age. We need not enumerate the myriad structural

deficiencies which apparently plagued both vessels (US House Subcommittee, 1983:5). They may or may not have caused the accidents. The proponents of the vessel age theory are also standing on shaky epistemological ground. They too have placed their 'facts' together to meet their organizational, political and legal needs. Still their accounts are reasonable, at least as reasonable as those offered by the Coast Guard and the NTSB. The Coast Guard, however, has chosen not to focus its investigative efforts on the *Poet*'s badly corroded ballast tanks or the *Marine Electric*'s wasted hatch covers, and has denied any allegations that the vessels were unseaworthy. Its own inspectors, however, had checked and approved both vessels just months before their respective founderings. It has not responded to allegations that the inspectors assigned to both vessels were poorly trained. Apparently, the *Poet*'s last Coast Guard inspection was performed by a Philadelphia police officer who worked as a Coast Guard reservist every third weekend (US House Subcommittee, 1981:4). The Coast Guard inspector who boarded the *Marine Electric* testified that he did not know how to inspect hatch covers (US House Subcommittee, 1983:6-7)."

Tasca wrote his thesis in 1990, 25 years before the 40-year old *El Faro* was lost with all hands. The Coast Guard held the Marine Board of Inquiry into the *El Faro* sinking and loss, and their report was published on September 24, 2017. They delivered a lengthy list of conclusions, not one of which mentioned the age of the *El Faro* as a contributing factor. The only allusion to the ship's age was a passing reference to "vintage vessels like the *El Faro*." However, they did refer to the effectiveness of the Coast Guard's Alternative Compliance Program ("ACP") in section 8.7 of the Marine Board of Inquiry ("MBI"). They made 17 separate statements that highlighted the shortcomings of the ACP:

> "After encountering ACP related concerns during the EL FARO investigation, the MBI expanded the scope of its investigation to examine ACP effectiveness for EL YUNQUE and several other US flagged vessels enrolled in the program. After the sinking of EL FARO, the Coast Guard Traveling Inspectors began a focused effort to ascertain the material condition of the ACP vessels targeted by Office of Commercial Vessel Compliance. In addition, several Coast Guard field units reached out to the Traveling Inspectors for assistance with ACP vessels that were

known to be operating in a substandard safety condition starting in early 2015 and accelerating after the loss of EL FARO... In general, the ACP is not currently functioning as envisioned when the Program was created in 1996. The primary shortfalls observed over the course of the MBI include the following:

• An ACP training course for ACS [Authorized classification society = American Bureau of Shipping 'ABS'] surveyors and Coast Guard inspectors to interact and become familiar with the Program was never implemented.

• ACS surveyors and Coast Guard inspectors are often unfamiliar with the program requirements and the US Supplement.

• The US Supplement for ABS is not being updated on an annual basis and marine inspector identified gaps [e.g., the lack of hydrostatic testing requirements for propulsion boiler repairs] are not being incorporated into the Supplement updates.

• ACS surveyors and Coast Guard inspectors rarely interact in the field during ACP activities and there is no required minimum level of Coast Guard oversight required.

• There is no minimum qualification level required for Coast Guard personnel to conduct ACP oversight exams.

153

• The Coast Guard does not require marine inspectors to be trained as auditors.

• ABS training requirements for certain inspections activities [e.g., overseeing repairs to a propulsion steam boiler] are far less than the Coast Guard would require for a marine inspector conducting a similar inspection activity.

• ACS surveyors performing ACP inspections are reluctant to hold up a commercial vessel especially for observations that are outside the scope of the survey being performed.

• Coast Guard OCMIs [Officer in Charge, Marine Inspections] often lack the Prevention experience necessary to make time sensitive decisions to hold up substandard ACP vessels that have been cleared to operate by the ACS—a problem that is exacerbated by the limited number of Jones Act vessels available to perform certain trade routes.

• The Coast Guard Traveling Inspectors are encountering numerous long-standing safety deficiencies when they attend inspections on targeted ACP vessels which have frequently led to those vessels receiving no-sail orders.

• ACS surveyors are not held accountable for performing substandard ACP inspections that miss glaring safety deficiencies and the Coast Guard Office of Commercial Vessel Compliance does not have a system in place to associate an ACS with a substandard inspection they conduct on behalf of the Coast Guard.

• The Coast Guard does not publish an annual report on ACP vessel compliance or ACS performance. The lack of transparency has enabled vessel compliance and surveyor performance issues to continue unabated.

• The Coast Guard MISLE [Marine Information for Safety and Law Enforcement] database is not available to ABS surveyors and they are often unaware of outstanding requirements and special notes on the vessels they are surveying.

• The Coast Guard MISLE database is not designed to record and track the results of CG auditing activities.

• A formal Coast Guard course for advanced and specialized marine inspections [e.g., steam propulsion plants] is not available and the Coast Guard Center of Expertise that previously covered Vintage Vessels like the EL FARO was disbanded around 2012.

• The Liaison Officer for the Recognized and Authorized Class Societies [LORACS] billet at Coast Guard Headquarters that previously provided ACSs with a single point of contact for ACP related issues was eliminated in 2012.

• The ACP does not have a designated lead office or individual at Coast Guard Headquarters. As a result, multiple offices share responsibility for overseeing different aspects of the ACP which leads to confusion. Based on the results of the Coast Guard Traveling Inspector ACP oversight exams that were conducted in 2015 and 2016, it is clear that multiple US cargo vessels were operating for prolonged periods in a substandard material condition. Although the Coast Guard's focused oversight on the ACP targeted vessels corrected the most egregious cases of non-compliance, a seminal change in the overall management and execution of the Program is urgently needed to ensure safe conditions are sustained on the enrolled US commercial vessels."

In 1990, Tasca highlighted the problems of Coast Guard inspectors not being competent to conduct inspections. This point was raised by the Marine Board of Inquiry into the sinking and loss of the *Marine Electric*. Captain Calicchio, a member of the three-person panel, campaigned for the Coast Guard to put in place a new Coast Guard inspection team made up of experienced merchant mariners.

156

The *Marine Electric* Marine Board of Inquiry made 14 recommendations. Recommendation #2 stated: "That the Commandant commission a panel to conduct an in-depth review of the entire Coast Guard Commercial Vessel Safety Program and make recommendations to him. The panel should consist of no less than 50 percent retired Officers in charge, Marine Inspection recognized for their vessel inspection expertise, and recognized for their Merchant Marine background. The program's overall structure and the Coast Guard's ability to continue with such a program should be studied, with emphasis placed on:

a. The present and projected experience level of the program administrators, program and project managers, Officers in Charge, Marine inspection, and field inspectors, and the distribution of such expertise within the program.

b. The present and projected procurement and training programs, and identification of the requirements and qualifications needed of a marine inspector.

c. The review of all Headquarters, District, and field office policies and practices to detect any variation from statute or regulation."

Following a Marine Board of Inquiry, the report is forwarded to the commandant for review. The commandant of the Coast Guard has the authority to accept or reject the findings and recommendations of the Marine Board of Inquiry. Admiral J. S. Gracey rejected three out of the 14 recommendations made by the Marine Board of Inquiry. Admiral Gracey did not concur with recommendation number two stating that, "Efforts commenced before and after this tragic casualty are already addressing the mentioned issues... In view of these efforts establishment of a panel for the purpose recommended is not necessary."

Admiral Gracey also rejected recommendation number one, which stated:
> "That the examination of US merchant vessels to assure their compliance with the applicable Federal safety statutes and regulations be conducted and determined by knowledgable members of a US Government agency. The responsibilities for these functions should not be delegated or entrusted to the private sector."

Admiral Gracey's response stated in part:
> "As previously stated, the poor quality of the American Bureau of Shipping surveys in question cannot be justifiably expanded to condemn the entire system of third-party

delegation. What this casualty does support is the need for a more formalized oversight program by the Coast Guard."

The third rejection was recommendation number five, where the Marine Board of Inquiry stated:
"That the drydocking and Inspection for Certification be combined inspections for vessels over 100 gross tons."

Admiral Gracey responded as follows:
"While it may be more efficient to perform both inspections at the same time, there are valid reasons why vessel owners are unable to schedule concurrent inspections. In fact, separate inspections provide the Coast Guard with the opportunity for more frequent, thorough inspections of a vessel."

The late Captain Calicchio, one of the three members of the Marine Board of Inquiry into the loss of the *Marine Electric*, was interviewed by one of the reporters from the Philadelphia Inquirer. This interview took place many years after the inquiry, In his book *Until the Sea Shall Free Them*, Bob Frump quotes Captain Calicchio as saying, "If nothing else, I suppose we put a scare into the inspection system and the American Bureau of Shipping certainly cleaned up its act as a result." Captain Calicchio recognized during the Marine

Board of Inquiry that one of the root causes behind the sinking and loss of the *Marine Electric* was the failure of the inspection system both by his own employer the Coast Guard, and the party that the Coast Guard had contracted to perform inspections, the American Bureau of Shipping. Calicchio, as a former merchant mariner master, understood better than any other person on the panel the systemic failure that had allowed the *Marine Electric* to be sailing in such a poor state. He was well aware that the owners and their attorneys were doing their best to hide behind the privity of knowledge defense. The same systemic issues that were made transparent in January 1985 when the *Marine Electric* report was published were not acted on, and the proof of this came when the *El Faro* sank on October 1, 2015. These are evident in the findings published in the Marine Board of Inquiry into the sinking and loss of the *El Faro*.

The act and practice of cabotage create an environment of protectionism that is fueled by the special interest groups who stand to gain by its continuance. The lobbying of the US Congress to maintain cabotage is done under the guise of assisting the US Maritime Industry. The Coast Guard now operates under the Department of Homeland Security and is dependent on Congress for funding all of its programs. These programs include the oversight of the US Merchant Marine.

There is therefore a connective thread between those interests that seek to maintain cabotage and the government agency that is charged with oversight of its activities. For Captain Calicchio this meant holding firm on the findings and recommendations that had been sent to the commandant Admiral Gracey. Calicchio believed in one simple principle—To aid those in peril on the sea. After the report had been submitted to the commandant, Calicchio received a call from his mentor Admiral Lusk. In his book *Until the Sea Shall Free Them* Bob Trump quotes the conversation between Admiral Lusk and Calicchio as follows:

> "The general argument made to Calicchio by Lusk went like this: The real sticklers are your first two recommendations. You say we should get rid of the American Bureau of Shipping? And remove the Coast Guard entirely from inspections because they've been so bad? Turn it over to some new Agency?... Put something in a footnote. It looks bad for the Coast Guard, the way you have this. You know what the climate is in Washington. They want to outsource us completely!"

Calicchio stood firm and would not withdraw. This led to a lengthy delay in the release by the commandant. Calicchio's career with the Coast Guard was on the line. Calicchio knew that the

Marine Electric went down because the system that he was a part of had failed the 30 men that died. In December of 1984, Calicchio made his final move. He informed the chairman of the panel, Captain Lauridsen, that if the commandant did not release the report in January 1985, he would release the report publicly by sending it to the *Philadelphia Inquirer*. In January 1985, Admiral Gracey issued the report as written but the key recommendations concerning inspections were set aside by the commandant. Calicchio lost all hope of future promotion or status with the Coast Guard and he took his retirement in 1985. After the Coast Guard years, he became a consultant serving as an expert witness in court cases. Captain Calicchio passed on January 7, 2003.

In the Coast Guard's official blog there is a posting by Lt. Katie Braynard made on February 25, 2016, titled; "The Long Blue Line: Domenic Calicchio—Champion of marine safety regulations."
The posting by Braynard reads as follows:
        "Domenic A. Calicchio was one of the US
        Coast Guard's many unsung heroes whose
        career embodied the Service's core values of
        honor, respect and devotion to duty. The
        Coast Guard's Inspections & Investigation
        School named the Calicchio Award for him
        due to the significant impact he had on the
        US marine industry and the Coast Guard as

a senior marine casualty investigator... Throughout his Coast Guard career, Calicchio championed the cause of safety on the open ocean. Ironically, he downplayed his own critical role in overhauling marine safety regulations in the *Marine Electric* case and other marine safety cases during his Coast Guard career. Not long after the *Marine Electric* Marine Board released its critical 1985 report, Calicchio chose to retire. He went on to establish a successful practice as a cruise-ship safety expert in Fort Lauderdale, Florida. Calicchio was a member of the long blue line and his high regard for those who go to sea in ships set the standard for Coast Guard men and women tasked with overseeing marine safety."

In 1984, Captain Calicchio was a lone voice fighting for change because he was passionate about the loss of life on the *Marine Electric*. He campaigned for what he believed in. He paid a price because his battle against Commandant Gracey cost him his career. Thirty-two years later the Coast Guard cited him as one of their unsung heroes and named an award after him. They described him as a champion of safety. When the Marine Board of Inquiry issued their report into the sinking and loss of the *El Faro* in 2017 Captain Calicchio would recognize the following recommendations. They were echoes of his own words from 1984:

> Recommendation #26—Competency for Marine Inspections and ACS Surveyors Conducting Inspections on Behalf of the Coast Guard. It is recommended that Commandant direct the addition of an Advanced Journeyman Inspector course to the Training Center Yorktown curriculum. The course should cover ACS oversight, auditing responsibilities, and the inspection of unique vessel types. The course should be required for senior Coast Guard Marine Inspectors and made available to ACS surveyors who conduct inspections on behalf of the Coast Guard.

> Safety Recommendation #30—Third Party Oversight National Center of Expertise. It is recommended that Commandant consider creation of a Third-Party Oversight National Center of Expertise to conduct comprehensive and targeted oversight activities on all third-party organizations and ACSs that perform work on behalf of the Coast Guard. The Center of Expertise should be staffed with Subject Matter Experts that are highly trained inspectors, investigators, and auditors with the

capability and authority to audit all aspects of third-party organizations. As an alternative, the Coast Guard could add a new Third-Party Oversight Office at Coast Guard Headquarters with a similar staffing model as the proposed Center of Expertise. The new Third-Party Oversight Office could function similar to the Traveling Inspector Office and report directly to the Assistant Commandant for Prevention Policy."

Sadly, it has taken the loss of the *El Faro* to bring forward the same recommendations that Captain Calicchio had championed in 1984. We can only speculate about the course of events had Commandant Gracey accepted the recommendations of Calicchio in 1984. A more stringent inspection regime using properly trained inspectors would have discovered the *El Faro* to be unfit for service in the same way that they did when the traveling team of inspectors boarded the *El Yunque*. The *El Yunque* was the sister ship to the *El Faro* and they both operated on the Jacksonville to Puerto Rico service. After the loss of the *El Faro* on October 1, 2015, there is reason to believe that the Coast Guard, ABS and the owners TOTE might have accelerated their oversight of *El Yunque*. This was covered in the Marine Board of Inquiry, and the story shows that even after the loss of the *El Faro* the systemic faults remained in place.

"On February 1, 2016, three Coast Guard Traveling Inspectors attended EL YUNQUE as part of an ISM DOC Annual Audit of TOTE, which took place in Jacksonville, Florida. ABS led the DOC audit and provided three auditors, including the District Principal Surveyor. A Sector Jacksonville Coast Guard Marine Inspector also attended the audit as an observer. The Coast Guard does not normally participate in DOC audits; however, the Coast Guard Traveling Inspectors requested to be added to the team for TOTE's audit due to the previously identified maintenance concerns and the sinking of EL FARO four months earlier. Part of the DOC audit included a general walk-through of EL YUNQUE, and the Traveling Inspectors requested that TOTE open up a starboard exhaust ventilation trunk serving cargo Hold 3 for inspection. The Traveling Inspectors noted severe corrosion within the ventilation trunk and they subsequently conducted testing of the soundness of the internal structure of the trunk. This test, which was performed in a typical manner using a hammer, resulted in a hole through baffle plating that was required to be watertight (see Figure 27). As the Traveling Inspectors were discussing expansion of their inspection to additional ventilation trunks, the senior Traveling Inspector received a cell phone call from the Sector Jacksonville Commanding Officer. The Sector Commander, as the OCMI for the Port of Jacksonville, ordered the Traveling Inspectors to stop further inspection and hammer testing of EL YUNQUE's ventilation trunks because it exceeded the scope of the DOC audit; the Traveling Inspectors complied with that order. However, the Senior Traveling Inspector suspected that the potential for longstanding corrosion existed for the other ventilation trunks and voiced a concern that the wastage could present a down flooding risk if the vessel experienced severe rolls. As a result, the Traveling Inspectors requested that Sector Jacksonville conduct a follow-up inspection to check additional trunks for conditions similar to that of Hold 3's starboard exhaust vent trunk.

Under ACP protocols, Sector Jacksonville's Marine Inspector conferred with ABS and requested they oversee repairs to the ventilations trunks for Hold 3, check the condition of the other ventilation trunks, and issue conditions of class as necessary. ABS concurred with the Marine Inspector's concerns and required de-scaling and temporary repairs to the ventilation trunk casings that were identified as corroded during the DOC audit. On February 2, 2016, ABS surveyed temporary repairs to the holed and wasted areas in way of the port and starboard exhaust ventilation trunks for Hold 3146 including the following items:

- The lower 24" of the louver chamber's inboard bulkhead was cropped and renewed.
- An opening around the side shell longitudinal angle in the transverse baffle plate was closed.
- Drainage holes on both port and starboard trunks (smaller and larger) were satisfactorily closed up.

The ABS surveyor gave TOTE 30 days, until March 2, 2016, to make permanent repairs to the Hold 3 ventilation ducts and EL YUNQUE continued to operate between Jacksonville and San Juan. On February 9, 2016, ABS advised Sector Jacksonville that the temporary repairs had been completed to EL YUNQUE's port and starboard ventilation trunks that were identified as corroded on February 1, 2016. In March 2016, TOTE relocated EL YUNQUE to Seattle, Washington and started the process of converting the vessel back to its original RO/RO configuration for Alaskan service.

From March 18 to August 14, 2016, Coast Guard Sector Puget Sound Marine Inspectors made several visits to EL YUNQUE and, despite the February 2016, ABS survey and testimony from the ABS surveyor, recorded the following pertinent findings:

- April 6-12, 2016: Directed extensive third-party gauging for multiple suspect locations on the main deck. Found evidence of long-standing and uncorrected wastage.
- May 20, 2016: Examined supply vents for the Holds 1-3 port and starboard (6 total). Observed gaskets missing; holes in vent ducts; gasket flanges wasted; and holes in the side shell in way of vent inlets (see figure 28). Required all items to be added to the work list.
- August 14, 2016: TOTE halted work and requested to place the vessel in a lay-up vessel to be scrapped.
- December 23, 2016: Received notification that the vessel arrived at Brownsville, TX. Changed vessel status to "scrapped" in the Coast Guard's MISLE database.

From the facts presented we see that it took more than six months for the owners TOTE to realize that the *El Yunque* was no longer fit for service, and after 11 months the *El Yunque* was scrapped. The troubling part of this story is the fact that the Coast Guard Traveling Inspectors were ordered to stand down by their Jacksonville superiors during the February inspection. What reason would the Coast Guard senior commander in Jacksonville have for ordering the Coast Guard Traveling inspection team to stand down when they had clearly discovered a serious deficiency? These new findings not falling within the scope of the Document of Compliance "DOC" audit being conducted by ABS should have been irrelevant. The Traveling Inspectors had discovered a serious issue that affected seaworthiness, and this should have been actioned immediately, not deferred for some later action. What reason would the senior commander in Jacksonville have to take this position given the recent loss of the *El Faro*? Notably, after the *El Yunque* had been sent to the West Coast, the Coast Guard district at Puget Sound took a more stringent approach, and by August TOTE surrendered and declared that the *El Yunque* would be withdrawn and scrapped, thus ending the saga of the three PONCE class sisters. The *El Morro* and the *El Yunque* were both withdrawn as a result of extensive corrosion that failed inspections. The *El Faro* suffered the worst outcome, by sinking, according to the inquiry due to flooding through the open and corroded ventilators.

The story of the *El Faro* revolves around two key elements: cabotage, the system of protection which has led to a diversion of the Coast Guard's primary responsibility to mariners; and the Calicchio paradigm. The Calicchio paradigm is the dedication of an individual to be a champion for safety, in an expression of individual mindfulness even when the system or collective mindfulness is fully opposed to it. Cabotage has led to a powerful lobby of US Congress to maintain protection in order to benefit certain interests, and they assert this position by lobbying and donating to politicians. The US Congress has oversight over the Coast Guard budget and therefore the commandant of the Coast Guard has to appease those that control the funding. This leads Coast Guard to adopt a political response when addressing the recommendations of an inquiry. A Marine Board of Inquiry should be concerned only with findings of fact and cause, with the outcome being lessons learned without regard to politics.

Captain Dominic Calicchio did not succumb to commercial or political pressure and he sacrificed his career with the Coast Guard to deliver the right report. There are many Calicchios who stand up for the right thing. When they are not listened to or face retribution for their stand they may be forced to stand down. Some aspiring Calicchios are unable to risk forfeiting their livelihood to do what is right, and they are forced to submit to commercial pressure, accepting a compromise that they hope will not lead to a tragedy. Safety should never be compromised in this way and the responsibility must rest with positive dialog led by those who have the authority. This includes the shore management team and the competent authorities who conduct oversight.

I understand the Calicchio paradigm. I experienced this several times during my career at sea. In 1976, I was summoned to the bridge on a Canadian ship shortly before arriving in port. The master pointed to the logbook and asked me to sign the section stating that we had conducted a Boat and Fire Drill. I refused to sign because no such drill had taken place. The master was extremely angry with me. I politely explained that I could not sign, but what I could do was to conduct a Boat and Fire Drill immediately. We entered the harbor with boats swung out, and fire hoses spraying, crew mustered with lifejackets on. Then I could sign. The master would not have asked me to sign if he had not done this with others as a routine.

On another occasion, I was chief mate loading iron ore at Sept Iles, Quebec and in charge of cargo and ballast operations. The master came on deck and without consulting me started giving orders to the quartermaster to start pumping ballast. The master was the commandant of the fleet and I was a newly promoted chief mate. I went up to the master and challenged his action. I asked him if he was relieving me of my duties. He looked shocked and said, "No." I then explained that I was responsible for cargo and ballast operations. I could either carry on or I could leave the deck and hand over to him, his choice. I knew that chain of command was important and I either had the responsibility or not. If both of us were seen to be giving orders, this would create confusion and possible mistakes. He looked at me and after a few minutes said, "You are in charge mate," and left the deck. From that time forward we had an excellent working relationship.

Since 2006, Coast Guard has conducted Port State Control inspections on all foreign flag ships calling at US Ports. Port State Control arose from a 1982 agreement in Europe called the Paris MoU. This was in response to the loss of the tanker *Amoco Cadiz* off the French Brittany coast due to a steering gear failure, which resulted in a grounding and massive pollution of the Brittany coast. Twenty-six countries are now signatories to the Paris MoU. The Paris MoU gathers information and shares the data via its website. It ensures that problem ships are identified, and if they fail to comply, they are banned. US Coast Guard Port State Control inspections are intensive and thorough, and Coast

Guard tracks and monitors compliance, publishing information on a website. Foreign seafarers know that when they call at a US port, they can expect a multi-person team from Coast Guard that will spend several hours inspecting every aspect of the ship, from documents to galley cleanliness to full Fire and Abandon ship drills. The Port State Control inspections only apply to foreign flagged ships—Coast Guard does not inspect US flag ships under the Port State Control program.

In the matter of the *El Faro*, TOTE, the Coast Guard and ABS had become infected with what Mr. Justice Sheen called the "disease of sloppiness." The master and crew had become complacent on their routine run to Puerto Rico. Captain Davidson was focused on being chosen to be the master of one of the new Marlin class ships and thus he exchanged his responsibility for safety in favor of trying to stay in a favorable light with TOTE's decision-makers. His prior experience with Crowley Maritime, which resulted in him losing his command due to ordering tugs because of a safety concern, no doubt weighed heavily on his decisions to set out on the shortest route to San Juan on September 29, 2015, directly into the path of Hurricane Joaquim. Davidson knew that the *El Faro's* stability was tender and that her ventilation scuttles were routinely left open and exposed to the sea. He probably did not know that the lubricating oil in the steam turbine sumps was lower and susceptible to losing suction if the *El Faro* took a list. None of this would have happened had TOTE properly maintained the *El Faro*. The oversight to ensure compliance rested with Coast Guard and ABS. There was systemic failure, the importance of which was flagged by Calicchio in 1984 following the loss of the *Marine Electric*. Had Commandant Gracey accepted all of the recommendations of the *Marine Electric* Marine Board of Inquiry, the inspection process would probably have been changed and made more stringent. The latent defects of the *El Faro* became greater as a result of her conversion and her age. Every mariner knows that as ships age they require more maintenance to combat corrosion and general wear and tear. In the case of the *El Faro* the skirts of cabotage kept the truth from being observed because nobody cared enough to observe them.

Nine: Stellar Daisy, 2017

On March 31, 2017, the Very Large Ore Carrier *Stellar Daisy*, loaded with a cargo of Brazilian sinter iron ore fines, sank in the South Atlantic Ocean. Of the 24 crew onboard, only two were rescued from a life-raft. Fourteen Filipino and eight South Korean seafarers did not survive the sinking. Two Filipinos managed to board a life-raft and were rescued by the Greek bulk carrier *Elpida* one day after the sinking. The testimony provided by the two Filipino seafarers, Renato Daymiel, engine room oiler, and Jose Cabrahan, deck AB seaman is available on the Facebook page website "Cool Merchant Mariners":

On February 17, 2019, the *Seabed Constructor* owned by Global Infinity found the wreck of the *Stellar Daisy* on the seabed at a depth of 3,461 meters.

The wreck is 1,800 miles west of Cape Town, South Africa. Global Infinity was hired by the South Korean government to find the *Stellar Daisy* and to recover the voyage data recorder. South Korea stepped forward to pay for the search and recovery because of the South Korean seafarers that were onboard.

In December 2018 the South Korean government signed a contract worth $4.3 million with Global Infinity. The *Stellar Daisy* was under the flag of the Marshall Islands and was owned by the South Korean company Polaris. The Korean News agency Yonhap quoted the families of the lost South Korean seafarers as follows: "We hope that there will not be any suspicion left about the sinking by ensuring that all processes [of verifying the truth] are conducted transparently."

On February 18, 2019, Global Infinity reported the recovery of the *Stellar Daisy's* voyage data recorder.

Under maritime law and convention, the flag state has the primary responsibility of conducting an investigation. In the case of the *Stellar Daisy* the ship was under the Marshall Islands flag and registry. The Marshall Islands (officially, the Republic of the Marshall Islands) is an island country in Micronesia located near the Equator just west of the International Date Line. The territory consists of some 29 coral atolls supporting a population of 53,000 people. The islands derive their name from the visit of British explorer John Marshall in 1788. During World War II, the United States took control of the Marshall Islands and has maintained a free association with the Republic. Under the Compact of Free Association, citizens of the Marshall Islands enjoy unrestricted access to reside and work in the USA. The Marshall Island ship registry began operating in 1990; however, all of the work associated with the management of the Marshall Island registry is managed by a US based firm, International Registries, Inc. ("IRI"), based in Reston, Virginia. The website of IRI describes their business as follows:

"International Registries, Inc. and its affiliates [IRI] provide administrative and technical support to the Republic of the Marshall Islands [RMI] Maritime and Corporate Registries. IRI has been administering maritime and corporate programs and involved in flag State administration since 1948. IRI has an excellent reputation within the international business community and will continue to be at the forefront of vessel, and corporate registration. IRI is the world's most experienced, privately held maritime and corporate registry service provider, recognizing the specialized needs of the shipping and financial services industries across a broad commercial and economic spectrum. Headquartered just outside of Washington, DC in Reston, Virginia USA, IRI operates 28 offices in major shipping and financial centers around the world."

Under the web page titled "Maritime Investigations," IRI states as follows:

"The RMI [Republic of Marshall Islands] Maritime Administrator [the 'Administrator'] conducts marine safety investigations of marine casualties and incidents to promote the safety of life and property at sea and to promote the prevention of pollution. Marine safety investigations do not seek to apportion blame or determine liability and are conducted according to the IMO Casualty Investigation Code with the objective of preventing marine casualties and marine incidents in the future."

The IRI website allows one to download prior investigations. The most notable report available is the April 2010 incident on the *Deepwater Horizon* in the Gulf of Mexico.

A notable feature of the investigation reports published by the Marshall Islands Administrator is that they do not identify the name of the person or persons leading the inquiry, or the names of assessors aiding the person or persons conducting the inquiry. The authors remain anonymous, and the report is issued only in the name of the Republic of the Marshall Islands Administrator. In the section of the report that deals with recommendations, there are sections that are written from the perspective of the Administrator, such as "The Administrator recommends..." There are other sections where, in contrast, the recommendations are directed to "the Administrator," such as "It is recommended that the Administrator present..." These different styles appear on the same page, making it difficult to understand if the report is authored by the anonymous "Administrator" or the voice of anonymous "others," presumably the staff at IRI who are writing on behalf of the Administrator. In the preamble to each investigation it states:

> "An investigation under the authority of Republic of the Marshall Islands laws and regulations, including all international instruments to which the Republic of the Marshall Islands is a Party, was conducted to determine the cause of the casualty."

This is followed by the official stamp of the "Office of the Maritime Administrator."

There is no identity given to the person who fulfills the role of the Maritime Administrator. In a Marine Notice issued about "Onboard Complaint Procedures" the notice provides that:

> "Inquiries concerning the subject of this Notice should be directed to the Office of the Maritime Administrator, Republic of the

Marshall Islands, c/o Marshall Islands Maritime and Corporate Administrators, Inc., 11495 Commerce Park Drive, Reston, VA 20191-1506 USA."

The notice states that: "The RMI Maritime Administrator's contact email address for such complaints is seafarers@register-iri.com." The Marshall Island Maritime Administrator appears to work from the IRI offices in Reston, Virginia. The identity of that person and their qualifications are not identified.

The International Maritime Organization ("IMO") has called on the Marshall Islands to conduct a full investigation under the authority of the "Code of the International Standards and Recommended Practices for a Safety Investigation into a Marine Casualty or Marine Incident."

> "'It is expected that there will be a full investigation into this accident and that the results and findings will be brought to IMO so that we can do whatever may be necessary to reduce the chances of such an incident happening again,' said IMO secretary general Kitack Lim in a statement. 'Thankfully these occurrences are rare; but when they do happen, they serve to remind everyone that the seafarers, on whom we all depend, do a difficult and sometimes dangerous job; and that those of us

responsible for making the industry safer can never stop striving for improvements.'"

The United Nations Convention on the Law of the Sea under article 94 stipulates the responsibilities of a flag state as follows:
"Each State shall cause an inquiry to be held by or before a suitably qualified person or persons into every marine casualty or incident of navigation on the high seas involving a ship flying its flag and causing loss of life or serious injury to nationals of another State or serious damage to ships or installations of another State or to the marine environment. The flag State and the other State shall co-operate in the conduct of any inquiry held by that other State into any such marine casualty or incident of navigation."

The South Korean government has funded the search for the wreck and the recovery of the voyage data recorder in response to the requests and lobbying from the families of the missing South Korean seafarers, and sensitivity to the strong South Korean connection with both the owners based in Seoul and the South Korean classification society. The impact of the April 2014 ferry *Sewol*, sinking off Jindo Island, and the 304 that died has remained in the public consciousness. A court hearing in

Seoul in January 2019 rejected an arrest warrant for a Korean Register of Shipping ("KR") surveyor in connection with the loss of the *Stellar Daisy*. This prompted KR to make the following statement:

> "The safety of lives and safeguarding the marine environment are top priorities for KR and the society will continue to work with all the relevant authorities to assist with the investigation into the tragic loss of this vessel."

The *Stellar Daisy* was classed with the Korean Register of Shipping. KR had approved the conversion of the *Stellar Daisy* from a Very Large Crude Carrier to a Very Large Ore Carrier. The conversion work took place in China at the Zhoushan shipyard after Polaris Shipping acquired the VLCC tanker *Sunrise III* in 2006. The converted *Stellar Daisy* entered service in 2008. The *Sunrise III* had been built at the Nagasaki shipyard in Japan and entered service as a tanker in July 1993. Polaris Shipping, based in Seoul, recognized a commercial opportunity to acquire four single-hulled VLCC tankers and convert them into ore carriers. Changing regulations under the Oil Pollution Act meant that single-hulled tankers were being phased out in favor of double-hull tankers. The concept was straightforward: the center tanks would become the new holds for the carriage of iron ore. The center tanks would be fitted with a new floor constructed to create a double bottom tank underneath the cargo hold. Hatch openings, coamings and hatch covers would be fitted for loading and discharging. The former side tanks would remain for use as ballast tanks. There were many such conversions of single-hulled VLCC tankers to VLOC ore carriers—so much so that the London based Protection and Indemnity (PandI) insurer Steamship Mutual issued a special publication in 2008 on their website. Steamship Mutual provides a detailed overview of the conversion process and the commercial reasons that support the work:

> "The attraction for owners of sending their VLCCs for conversion is easily seen when the cost of converting a VLCC will generally be paid off in 1 to 2 years at present charter rates and with a bullish outlook for the dry bulk market. However, the impact on charter rates of the influx of over 550 cape-size bulk carriers, due to be delivered over the next five years, remains to be seen."

Under the section "Statutory Requirements," Steamship Mutual states the following:

> "The change from a tanker to a bulk carrier gives rise to compliance issues with a number of statutory requirements. The principal change is from a type A vessel to a type B vessel under the Load Line

Convention and due to the vessel lifting a similar weight of cargo as to when she was a VLCC the waterline will be similar to previously. This give rise to issues with the minimum bow height and reserve buoyancy forward.

This can be overcome by fitting a raised forecastle, which in itself is no easy task allowing for the modifications to the chain lockers and lifting the windlass, mooring winches and mooring furniture by a deck. A further complication can be that the raising of the forecastle interferes with the IMO visibility requirements from the bridge looking past the forecastle, this may also require an increase in the height of the bridge to ensure the visibility past the forecastle is kept within requirements. The class requirements for the fitting of raised forecastles on bulk carriers, OBO's and OO's does not seem to apply, as the Class requirement makes no mention of conversions post the date of implementation."

The Steamship Mutual comment about the fitting of a raised forecastle reflects back to earlier chapters and the case of the *Derbyshire* and the *Marine Electric*. Both ships had no raised forecastle to provide protection to their foredeck hatch covers.

An article published in the May 2017 issue of the Royal Institute of Naval Architects magazine *The Naval Architect*, titled "Lessons must be learned from ore carrier sinking," sheds light on the potential defects. The article is written by Sandra Speares. Speares begins by saying that: "The tragic loss of Polaris Shipping's *Stellar Daisy* is under investigation, and the structural viability of the whole VLOC fleet looks set to come under the spotlight." Speares continues and draws attention to the question of liquefaction of the iron ore fines as a possible cause. Speares writes:

"Liquefaction has received increasing attention as a result of casualties like *Bulk Jupiter* in 2015 and initial comment suggested this might be the cause of the *Stellar Daisy* casualty. In the weeks since the accident the focus has turned to the dangers of converting ships designed for one trade to another, for example from VLCC to VLOC."

Intercargo, the International Association of Dry Cargo Shipowners, on their website describe their function as follows:

"[INTERCARGO] was established in 1980 with the objective of giving a voice to shipowners, managers and operators of dry cargo vessels and represent better this shipping sector. The power of

INTERCARGO, like its partner shipping associations, is that collectively, it is possible to change bulk carrier industry for the better in a world where one bulk carrier shipowner acting on its own finds it most difficult to make itself heard and facilitate progress."

On January 31, 2019, Intercargo issued a media release titled "Cargo liquefaction continues to be a major risk for dry bulk shipping." They made the following statement:

"Moisture related cargo failure mechanisms, widely known as liquefaction, continue to be a major concern for dry bulk shipping. Although there has been no reported loss of life or loss of ship attributed to liquefaction in 2018, INTERCARGO urges all stakeholders to remain vigilant as cargo liquefaction continues to pose a major threat to the life of seafarers."

"Ship operators need to be especially cautious when loading during a wet season, as currently being experienced in certain parts of South East Asia, however it is paramount that the shippers and the local authorities fulfil their obligations as required by the IMSBC Code."

"INTERCARGO's annually produced Casualty Report highlights the tragic loss of life associated with liquefaction. The last report for the years 2008-2017 showed that 101 lives and 9 bulk carriers were likely lost due to cargo failure (this compared with a total of 202 lives lost in all 53 casualties). Those 9 bulk carrier losses comprised 6 vessels loaded with nickel ore from Indonesia, 2 vessels with laterite (clay) iron ore from India, and 1 with bauxite from Malaysia."

Four of the ships covered in this book were subject to conversions. The *Marine Electric* was converted from a T2 tanker to a bulk carrier, the *Sewol* was converted to increase passenger space, the *El Faro* was converted from a pure roll-on roll-off to also carry lift-on lift-off containers on deck, and the *Stellar Daisy* went from a crude oil tanker to an ore carrier. In my experience, converted ships represent a compromise in design, as the process of adapting means accepting changes. I sailed on a British bulk carrier that had initially been a tanker. As a tanker, steam was needed for tank heating, tank cleaning and for the steam turbine pumps. The tanker was fitted with a slow-speed marine diesel engine for propulsion, but a large auxiliary boiler provided steam for operations. When the conversion took place, the decision was made to fit steam cargo winches at each cargo hold rather than electric winches. During lengthy port operations, this required large amounts of steam to be generated and the boiler was always on. Electric winches would have only used power when they operated, and thus been much more efficient and required far less maintenance. The only advantage to our steam winches was the warmth they provided to winch operators during the winter months. The same ship had to be fitted with riveted doubling plates along the main deck on either side of the midships accommodation due to weakness in the deck plating, most likely due to the change from the longitudinal framing of the tanker hull to the transverse framing of the bulk carrier design.

The *Stellar Daisy* was also 24 years old when she sank in the South Atlantic. To get a sense of the age of deep-sea ships, you can use the same rule of thumb people use with horses to understand their age in "human years": multiply by three. Applying this rule, a five-year-old ship is like a fifteen-year-old teenager, a ten-year-old ship is a 30-year-old young adult. By 20 years the ship is beginning its senior years. The *Stellar Daisy* was 72 in human years, so definitely a senior and therefore well into the aging process. This explains why special periodic surveys required by Classification Societies take place at 5-year intervals. The intensity of the periodic surveys intensifies as the ship reaches the 20-year survey and beyond. As they pass beyond the third periodic survey, special attention is given to non-destructive testing using ultrasonic equipment to measure the effects of corrosion. The cost of replacing wasted steel is very expensive for ship owners and often becomes a cost-benefit analysis for ending the operational life of a ship. Only during periods of very bullish freight markets can the cost of replacement steel be justified.

The oldest ship that I sailed on was the *Canadian Transport*, an ore carrier built in 1954. She was 22 years old when I served on her as chief officer. At the time she was the largest ship under the Canadian flag. The *Canadian Transport* was scrapped in 1978 after 24 years of operational service.

Any merchant mariner will be wary of any ship that is 20 years old or older. The Lloyd's insurance market recognizes 15 years as the working life, and after 15 years they charge a supplemental insurance premium known as "over-age insurance." Many charterers will not accept the nomination of a ship that is considered over-age at the time of loading. The 15-year threshold corresponds to 45 years using the 3:1 formula. Perhaps Lloyd's see this as the time of mid-life crisis in the age of a merchant ship.

Iron ore is the key ingredient for the global steelmaking industry, and it is shipped in several forms. It can be a processed ore that is compressed into a round pellet, fines that are dark brown or black, or lump ore with larger sized pieces. The nature of the ore depends on the source. Iron ore is sold on the percentage of the pure iron that the ore contains and adjusted for the amount of moisture it contains. Steel companies are the buyers of iron ore, and they purchase a blend of ores to achieve the most efficient combination for their blast furnaces. Buyers search for the optimum mix of price versus the "Fe" content and pay the shippers on a dry weight basis. Pellets are the premium product, and the price is therefore much higher on a per ton basis. The fines, particularly those loaded in Brazil, have higher moisture content. The ore is stored in outside yards, and so during the rainy season, the ore absorbs moisture. The moisture content is a serious concern to mariners because of the risk of liquefaction, a condition in which the ore can transform itself from a solid to a slurry. The International Solid Bulk Cargoes Code ("ISMBC") describes the condition as follows:

> *7.2.4.* In the resulting viscous fluid state cargo may flow to one side of the ship with a roll but not completely return with a roll the other way. Consequently, the ship may progressively reach a dangerous heel and capsize quite suddenly.

I had experience loading a cargo of Canadian ore fines on a Panamax self-unloader called the *Phosphore Conveyor* and have seen for myself the vast amount of water that literally bleeds from the cargo. In our case, underneath the cargo holds we had a centerline tunnel that carried a conveyor belt system. The hydraulic gates that were used to feed the cargo on the conveyor were not designed to be watertight, so gravity caused the water to seep down through the gates and into the tunnel. On the first day at sea as we headed to Mobile, Alabama, I found the tunnel flooded. We had the bilge pumps running non-stop through the entire voyage to keep up with the steady flow of water coming from the cargo.

The *Derbyshire* had loaded Carol Lake concentrates at Sept Iles, Quebec in 1980 on her final voyage to Japan. The book *Return of the Coffin Ships* by Bernard Edwards stated that the reported moisture content was 3.6%, and that translates to 5,668 tons of water that would have been steadily filling the bilges of the *Derbyshire*'s holds. At the Formal Inquiry, liquefaction was not considered to be a root cause of the *Derbyshire*'s demise.

Susan Gourvenec, Professor of Offshore Geotechnical Engineering at the University of Southampton, published an article on August 29, 2018, titled: "Mystery of the cargo ships that sink when their cargo suddenly liquefies." Gourvenec describes the process of liquefaction with great clarity, writing:

> "A solid bulk cargo that is apparently stable on the quayside can liquefy because pressures in the water between the particles build up as it is loaded onto the ship. This is

especially likely if, as is common practice, the cargo is loaded with a conveyor belt from the quayside into the hold, which can involve a fall of significant height. The vibration and motion of the ship from the engine and the sea during the voyage can also increase the water pressure and lead to liquefaction of the cargo."

"When a solid bulk cargo liquefies, it can shift or slosh inside a ship's hold, making the vessel less stable. A liquefied cargo can shift completely to one side of the hold. If it regains its strength and reverts to a solid state, the cargo will remain in the shifted position, causing the ship to permanently tilt or 'list' in the water. The cargo can then liquefy again and shift further, increasing the angle of list."

"At some point, the angle of list becomes so great that water enters the hull through the hatch covers, or the vessel is no longer stable enough to recover from the rolling motion caused by the waves. Water can also move from within the cargo to its surface as a result of liquefaction and subsequent sloshing of this free water can further impact the vessel's stability. Unless the sloshing can be stopped, the ship is in danger of sinking."

Gourvenec provides further insight when she describes the commercial pressures that are prevalent within the industry. Gourvenec explains as follows:

"Commercial agendas also play a role. For example, pressure to load vessels quickly leads to more hard loading even though it risks raising the water pressure in the cargoes. And pressure to deliver the same tonnage of cargo as was loaded may discourage the crew of the vessel draining cargoes during the voyage."

Gourvenec's two points about the pressure to load quickly and to deliver the bill of lading quantity at the discharge port are both valid.

During my career working in the steel industry every discharge terminal receiving iron ore fines and concentrates struggled with the consistency of the material. The wet and sticky ore attaches to transfer chutes on conveyor systems, creating blockages in the hoppers. At the end of the discharge, the bottom of the cargo holds become awash in a slurry of ore that makes the final part of the discharge extraordinarily messy and complicated. For ships' crews, the task of pumping out the water left behind and the tailings that remained underwater also creates major headaches because ore carriers have no cranes to lift out residual cargo. This creates a significant problem for the task of hold cleaning, especially with the smaller crew sizes in use today.

The problem in a standard bulk carrier is that the moisture can only be extracted via the ship's bilges. Bilges are recessed rectangular compartments located at the aft end of each hold. They sit inside the double bottom tank and below the floor or tank-top of the cargo hold. They are designed with two sections. One side has the access cover and grating that allows water to flow inside. Once water drains into the first section, there is a baffle plate that allows any solids to settle. As the level of water rises, it can then flow over the baffle plate into the second section which has the suction line to the bilge pump. To protect the first section from becoming filled with solids, the access grating is routinely covered with a layer of burlap cloth to act as a filter material protecting the first section of the bilge; the burlap is held in place with cement. In the case of ore concentrates the material itself is so fine that it can penetrate the burlap and fill the bilge compartment, potentially causing the bilge to become blocked with ore fines. Bilge compartments were a frequent visiting place during my years as a navigating cadet. Onboard British merchant ships the task of cleaning out bilge compartments and setting burlap and cement was a job reserved for the cadets. Bilge compartments are large enough to crawl inside, and after the discharge of a grain cargo they contain fermented grain that has been stimulated by the urine of stevedores who use the bilges as their toilet facility. Once we had cleaned out any solids from the bilge, we would dust the inside of the bilge with lime to "sweeten" the bilge and take away the foul odor.

When a ship moves and vibrates at sea, the phenomenon known as liquefaction can occur, and that can lead to the ore cargo behaving like a fluid. As the ship rolls and pitches, the liquefied cargo can then shift inside the hold dramatically, and—dangerously—the liquified mix is very dense and heavy. Once it is in motion, it can easily collapse a bulkhead or breach the hull plating. The moisture turns the relatively inert pile of ore into a live monster of angry liquid. The phenomenon of liquefaction has been witnessed ashore at the tailing ponds in Brazil, where vast volumes of liquefied iron ore tailings have breached their dams to create a widespread loss of life and damage to those living below the dams. The liquefied slurry was captured on video by a CCTV camera at the Brumadinho Dam failure in 2019. Imagine for a moment the danger that arises when a cargo of iron ore fines transforms itself into a liquified slurry within a ship's hold. Instead of being a static mass, the cargo is dynamic, swirling around the hold gathering energy as the ship rolls. Liquefaction is an even more significant consideration on larger bulk carriers where there is a greater area of free surface for the dynamic ore to go wild.

At this stage, without the data from the underwater survey and the VDR, we have limited knowledge. We do know from the testimony of the two survivors that there was a loud noise and the ship was listing fast to port. This suggests that either a port side ballast tank had become flooded by a rupture in the shell plating or that the sinter fines in a center cargo hold had ruptured the bulkhead and had poured into the port side tank. The latter explanation might explain the loud noise as the cargo crashed down into the side ballast tank, and it would certainly account for a steady and progressive list to port. The underwater survey should reveal more and enable forensic analysis to be made.

Following the example set by the Derbyshire Families Association, the families of the South Korean seafarers have come together to campaign for the truth. They have posted a video to YouTube entitled: "Appeal From The Families Of The Korean MV Stellar Daisy For Finding the Black

Box, Full Disclosure And Proper Health And Safety Protection For Seafarers" (https://www.youtube.com/watch?v=OZU3OoboXn w&feature=youtu.be).

Proactive action has been taken by the government of South Korea to contract Global Infinity to locate the wreck and to recover the voyage data recorder. This demonstrates that the flag state of the South Korean crew members has taken proper steps to understand what happened to the *Stellar Daisy*. Under the United Nations law of the sea discussed previously, the Marshall Islands has a legal obligation to conduct the investigation.

Casualty Investigation Report
On April 19, 2019, the Republic of the Marshall Islands Maritime Administrator published the "*Stellar Daisy* Casualty Investigation Report." In a footnote on the final page of the report, they state: "This includes information that might be recovered from *Stellar Daisy*'s S-VDR and shared with the administrator." We therefore know that the Marshall Islands Administrator published the report without the data from the voyage data recorder that was reported found two months earlier on February 18, 2019.

We know from the *Edmund Fitzgerald*, *Derbyshire*, *Marine Electric*, *Estonia* and the *El Faro* incidents that information from underwater surveys and voyage data recorders, where these have been fitted, have proven to be critical evidence in understanding the cause. In the report, the following statement is made (p. 43, footnote 138):

> "In February 2019, *Stellar Daisy* was located in approximate position 34° 22.8'S 018° 29.4'W during a deep-sea search conducted by the Republic of Korea. The Republic of Korea has provided the administrator a copy of the video that was taken during the search. This video has been taken into consideration as part of the Administrator's marine safety investigation."

Unfortunately, the Marshall Islands Administrator provides no details about the evidence provided by the video and how it relates to their findings. The report has been published without revealing the video evidence and without information from the voyage data recorder. The lack of disclosure by the Marshall Islands Administrator raises questions and will no doubt lead to calls for the investigation to be reopened to incorporate evidence from the voyage data recorder and the underwater survey. The voyage data recorder will provide critical evidence on the chronology of events, and the underwater survey will reveal the condition of the structure following the sinking.

The Marshall Islands Administrator Executive Summary stated that:

> "The likely direct cause of the *Stellar Daisy* foundering was a rapid list to port following a catastrophic structural failure of the ship's hull that resulted in a loss of buoyancy and uncontrolled flooding. The structural failure and flooding are thought to have begun in the No. 2 port water ballast tank (WBT) and then progressed rapidly to include structural failure and flooding in multiple WBTs, voids and cargo holds. The structural damage was likely due to a combination of factors, including the strength of the ship's structure being compromised over time due to material fatigue, corrosion, unidentified structural defects, multi-port loading, and the forces imposed on the hull as a result of the weather conditions *Stellar Daisy* encountered between 29-31 March 2017."

Notably, the keywords in the Executive Summary are "likely," and "thought to have." The findings in the report are based on the limited evidence available to the Maritime Administrator.

Cargo liquefaction is not stated as one of the factors in the Executive Summary because the Maritime Administrator has accepted the sampling data provided by the shipper as valid, even though they do raise concerns that third-party sampling is prohibited by the shippers.

Moisture Content and Bilges

The Maritime Administrator also accepts that the absence of water in the cargo bilges as an indication that the cargo was not an issue. However, they do not question how this can be true when the moisture content of the sinter fines was 9.23%. They do not consider that the cargo bilges could be blocked by fines clogging whatever filter material the *Stellar Daisy* had in place to protect the cargo bilges. On page 36, under item 74, they state: "In addition, the cargo wells [bilges] were likely fitted with a micro filtration system to prevent clogging of the bilge system by cargo particles." A footnote is added describing the shipper's recommendation to fit filtration, and statements from Polaris Shipping and a prior master that bilge wells were fitted with a filtration system. However, one of the survivors was an AB seaman, and there is no direct testimony from him about how the bilges were prepared. This is an important gap in evidence gathering from a person with direct knowledge. Interviews with the survivors must have taken place because the Administrator reports in section 77 that: "Further, the surviving crew members reported they were not aware of any problems that occurred during cargo loading."

Sinter fines are a notoriously wet cargo, and the 9.23% moisture content translates to 24,000 tons of water distributed throughout the cargo holds. However, since the ore fines were reclaimed from the stocking yards at the Ilha Guaiba terminal, there can be variances in moisture content depending on the condition existing in different areas of the stockpile being reclaimed. Bucket wheel reclaimers can be working various stockpiles and at alternating heights. There can be no certainty that the moisture content is constant throughout the loading.

The relatively small volume of the cargo bilges at 4.86 m³ each resulted in less than 10 m³ of bilge capacity for the No. 2 cargo hold, which had a total volume of 27,315 m³. On page 20, section 21, the report states: "These bilge wells could be drained directly to the centerline voids or emptied using a bilge pump." In the attached footnote it states:
> "The piping and valves for these drains are not included on the drawing of the bilge system, nor is it known whether they were fitted when the ship was converted to a VLOC or at a later date. It is noted that a void is commonly understood as a space or tank that is not used to hold oil, water, etc."

On page 29, section 46 (c) there is a statement as follows:

"The Masters observed that the apparent cause of the observed corrosion was the practice of draining water that accumulated in the cargo hold bilges into these voids after loading."

The Administrator does not show how they investigated the fitment of the bilge drains or the operating practices in use regarding draining bilge water into the center voids.

This information shows that the *Stellar Daisy* had problems with water coming from the cargo and they had fitted the special drains for a reason. One explanation not explored by the Marshall Islands Administrator is the possibility that, rather than pumping out the bilges, they may have drained water into the center voids (double bottoms). This then avoids a deadweight discrepancy between the bill of lading weight at the loading port and the outturn survey at the discharge port. By retaining the water onboard, the deadweight of the cargo remains constant. Professor Susan Gourvenec, from the Offshore Geotechnical Engineering department at the University of Southampton, cites this as a concern in her report published on August 29, 2018.

The practice of bilge water management is also relevant at the discharge port when the cargo holds are near empty. There is typically an excess of water in the cargo holds. As the water is dirty with iron ore, the bilges cannot be pumped into the harbor. In such cases, the ship has to pump the bilge water into a ballast tank. It is conceivable that the *Stellar Daisy* used the center tanks under the cargo holds as holding tanks for dirty bilge water. This is supported by the statement in section 46 (c).

Inspection

The Maritime Administrator reveals in the report that inspections undertaken, following the loss of the *Stellar Daisy*, on 11 converted VLOCs owned by Polaris Shipping identified numerous serious problems. The inspections took place between April and August 2017. These inspections noted the following and are stated in section 128 of the report as follows:

> a) Areas of fatigue were found on most of the ships.
> b) The under deck areas were a high-risk area on all of the ships.
> c) The rating of the coatings in the voids and WBTs on some of the ships as fair did not appear to be consistent with IACS guidance for assessing coating conditions.
> d) the structural repairs that had been made in the shipyard or as voyage repairs were generally: not based on any structural analysis, completed without a detailed repair plan, and commonly accomplished using short inserts; and

e) Voyage repairs were not consistently reported to the ship's Classification Society.

The list of problems revealed by the inspections of the 11 converted VLOCs following the loss of the *Stellar Daisy* shows that these ships have latent defects as a result of the conversion, the age and shortcomings in the inspection and survey during operations. This is similar to the case of the *El Faro* and the US Coastguard's subsequent inspection of the sister ship *El Yunque*.

In Part 6 of the Recommendations, the Maritime Administrator writes six recommendations to itself under recommendation section 3. The first one states: "review, and if deemed appropriate, revise its RO [Recognized Organization—Korean Register of Shipping] oversight procedures based on the lessons learned from this investigation." Here we see that the Marshall Islands Administrator is investigating and making recommendations to itself. This raises questions of whether the Maritime Administrator is "suitably qualified," as defined under article 94 of the United Nations Convention on the Law of the Sea.

Liquefaction
The report contains no details of the stowage plan showing the quantity of cargo loaded in each of the holds and the loading rotation that was followed.

These details should have been available from the loading terminal's records. The report is silent on this information except in section 78, when it cites the loading plan and details of the maximum bending and shear force. This information is missing from the Findings of Fact section. There is also no history of prior voyages carrying iron ore.

KR studied the effects of liquefaction at number 2 hold. On page 47, section 114, the report states the following:

> "KR determined that the scantlings for the longitudinal bulkhead plate and longitudinal and the transverse bulkhead plates and vertical stiffeners, while sufficient for a dry bulk cargo, were not sufficient to withstand the forces associated with a liquefied cargo."

KR also studied structural capability with a 45 degree list to port and a shift of cargo. On page 47, section 115, it is reported that KR found that "the longitudinal bulkheads could fail between transverse frames following a cargo shift."

The findings by KR reveal that the design scantlings were not capable of coping with a cargo experiencing liquefaction and that the longitudinal bulkheads would fail following a cargo shift.

Chronology

The report describes the chronology of events and focuses on two key elements, the 1320 report of the list and the 1325 EPIRB distress call. On page 40, under sections 86-91, there is a chronology of events that occurred on the afternoon of March 31. In section 89 the report states: "At 1320, a message was sent from *Stellar Daisy*'s Master to the ship's Superintendent reporting that No. 2 P WBT was flooding and that the ship was developing a rapid list to Port. No other details were provided."

In section 90 the report states: "At 1321, which was one minute after the message was sent to the ship's Superintendent reporting the No.2 P WBT flooding, a Digital Selective Calling [DSC] distress alert was sent from *Stellar Daisy*."

However, the message sent at 1320 reporting the event does not confirm whether this was the time that the flooding began or the time that the port list first began to develop. In practice, there would have been time between the actual event and the composing and sending of a message. Before sending such a serious message the master and senior officers would have been consulting and evaluating to understand the extent of the problem. One minute later the distress call was sent.

However, we know from the two survivors that several announcements were made over the ship's public address system summoning the crew to the bridge.

The AB reported in sections 91-94 that he went to his cabin, put on his immersion suit and lifejacket and went to his muster station on the port side. The AB then heard the master announce "All Crew go to the Bridge" twice on the ship's public address system. The AB went to the bridge using the outside port ladders. The sequence of events here shows that the AB had time to go to his cabin, put on an immersion suit and proceed to his muster station before he heard the public address announcement directing him to the bridge. Upon reaching the bridge, he found himself with many of the ship's company already assembled on the bridge. The AB observed the 3/O making a distress call on the VHF-FM radio. As this was taking place the AB saw green water entering the bridge through the door on the port side. The AB reported that the inclinometer showed a list of 45 degrees to port. The AB heard cracking and stated the ship rumbled like an earthquake. He then ran out of the port bridge door and jumped into the ocean.

The AB reported hearing the noise and was aware of the port list. He said this took place at 13:30 but that time is in doubt, unless local ship's time was different from the time reported in footnote 135 on page 40. Is it possible that the AB's watch had not been changed from the previous time zone of [GMT-2]? The *Stellar Daisy* was eastbound having left Brazil in the GMT-3 zone. The position of her loss placed the *Stellar Daisy* at 18 degrees 30.2 west longitude, which is nominally in the eastern portion of the GMT-2 time zone. In such case, the AB's watch may have shown 13:30 but ship's local time may have been 12:30. It is possible that the AB had not synchronized his watch to the most recent change in the ship's local time. This would then have allowed 55 minutes from the time the AB heard the noise to the EPIRB distress call. Given the AB's reported actions, this is a more likely scenario. However, we do not know what questions the Maritime Administrator asked of the two survivors. What is apparent is that data from the voyage data recorder will help to understand the chronology of events better and enable a more precise reconstruction.

Port List
The Maritime Administrator explores at great length the possible scenarios for the port list and the rapid capsizing, which they link to the flooding of number 2 port wing ballast tank. The hypothesis is that the flooding picked up by the sensors was external—seawater had penetrated the shell plating. However, another possibility is that the longitudinal bulkhead between number 2 cargo hold and number 2 port wing tank failed, causing water from the cargo to enter the WBT and trigger the sensors. When the bulkhead failed, there would have been an explosive noise as the bulkhead gave way with

the weight of the sinter fines. The weakness of the bulkhead is cited by KR, and the BSR report commissioned by the Maritime Administrator. The shockwave of sound within the empty and cavernous number 2 WBT would have created the noise that the AB heard. The effect of cargo shift would have created the vibrations felt by the oiler. The weight of the wet iron ore fines could then have slid into the ballast tank, causing the *Stellar Daisy* to "develop" a list ("develop" is the word that was used in the 13:20 message). However, it is probable that the noise heard by the AB and the oiler took place sometime before the report was sent at 13:20. As the list increased, the cargo in the other holds could have shifted to port, resulting in a further collapse of longitudinal bulkheads causing a continual list to port. The initial failure could have taken place in the way of number 2 and then cascaded like falling dominoes, as the latent defects of the catastrophic structural failure aligned to form the holes in the Swiss cheese. Once started, there was nothing to stop the complete roll over to port and sinking.

The report by the Marshall Islands Administrator reveals the existence of latent defects in the conversion of VLCCs to VLOCs. The 14 recommendations issued to the owners of the *Stellar Daisy* (Polaris Shipping), the Korean Register of Shipping and to the Maritime Administration of the

Marshall Islands represent a positive step forward to improve oversight of the VLOC fleet sailing under the Marshall Islands flag.

The *Stellar Daisy* was an over-aged ship, and it is clear from the previous chapters covering the *Marine Electric* and the *El Faro* that ships degrade as they age due to corrosion and fatigue. The need for inspection quality increases exponentially as the age of the ship increases. The physical task of inspecting huge ballast tanks and void spaces cannot be ignored. Access within the spaces is limited and difficult to assess fully. It takes many man-hours to climb around within frames. The Safety Management System "SMS" may stipulate quarterly inspections of tanks and voids with a checklist grading of five levels from excellent to poor. However, such a system of measurement is arbitrary and depends on the observer's view and how much time the observer spent within the space. Carriage of ore cargo like sinter fines with high moisture content does present operating challenges for the ship. Can the design of the bilges cope with the water, and how effective is the micro-filtration covering? The *Stellar Daisy* had a sophisticated bypass system that retained bilge water in the center tanks. The lack of water present in the bilges may not give an accurate indication of the amount of water present in the cargo holds.

The master and crew of the *Stellar Daisy* were not responsible for the design of the conversion from a VLCC. The weakness inherent in the structure and the effects of fatigue and corrosion were the latent defects ever-present as the *Stellar Daisy* sailed across the South Atlantic. The catastrophic structural failure either caused seawater to enter the wing ballast tank, or it may have allowed the ore cargo to shift. Whichever the case, both possibilities point to structural failure, and during the final hour of the *Stellar Daisy* the holes in her Swiss cheese aligned, with nothing available to prevent her growing list to port and sinking.

Ten: Connecting Threads

Professor James Reason wrote about "Foresight Training" in his book *Organizational Accidents Revisited*. The specific focus in that chapter was healthcare but, as he states, "Organizational Accidents have their origins in system weaknesses." To combat this he explains the need for mental skills to enhance risk awareness. Reason describes examples of how this can be implemented in the workplace and cites Esso's "Step Back Five by Five" program and Western Mining's "take time—take charge." In my safety training at Corus, we learned the Du Pont "Take Two" program. Each of these concepts is designed to create awareness through what Reason describes as "individual mindfulness." "Individual mindfulness" is supported by dialog and proactive near-miss reporting. Near-miss reporting allows the flow of information to be circulated so that issues are transparent rather than being suppressed. It is a vehicle that helps creative thought to flourish to encourage solutions to identify and correct a latent defect.

I have actively participated in the promotion of "individual mindfulness" in many workplace environments. I have always found it opens up dialog, and I have seen fresh ideas spring forward to resolve latent defects that had previously been considered normal. However, individual mindfulness can only flourish when there is an environment of collective mindfulness within the organization. Reason describes collective mindfulness as, "The Cultural change that empowers staff to step back from risky situations and seek help—where this is feasible." Sadly, what we find in all the eight chapters covering the 42-year period from the loss of the *Edmund Fitzgerald* to the *Stellar Daisy* is a failing in "Collective Mindfulness," and this leads to an open season for latent defects to be activated.

Looking at each of the eight losses, the principle connective thread is the failure of an environment of collective mindfulness from the shipowner. In some cases, these failures began during the design and building of the original hull. Notably, four of the eight (the *Marine Electric*, *Sewol*, *El Faro* and *Stellar Daisy*) had been subject to significant conversion work that had substantially altered their original design. In all the four that had been converted, the conversions themselves had created latent defects that would contribute to their demise.

The individual mindfulness of the crews responsible for operating each of the eight ships would always be limited in their ability to prevent slipping through the final hole of the Swiss Cheese Model. Captain McSorley and his crew on the *Edmund Fitzgerald* might have made another season had they not set off into the storm with the hatch covers not secure. Captain Underhill and the crew of the *Derbyshire* succumbed to a powerful wave beyond the strength of their ship. Captain Corl and the crew of the *Marine Electric* were sailing a ship that was not seaworthy. Captain Sabel and the crew of the *Herald of Free Enterprise* were so pressured by their schedule that they ignored the basic need to be watertight.

On the *Edmund Fitzgerald*, there was a culture of productivity to realize the maximum number of trips in the season, and there was no corresponding set of safeguards to ensure that safety was not compromised. Hatch covers were likely not fully secured, and they headed into the storm rather than waiting.

On the *Derbyshire*, the ship had been designed without any protection of her foredeck, leaving the crew at risk in a major storm. While abnormal waves were yet to be scientifically proven, mariners had reported their existence, but naval architects and builders had not been listening.

On the *Marine Electric*, the old bow and stern of a T2 tanker had been given a new midsection, but the new arrangement did not protect her foredeck. The owners had selectively looked away concerning the real condition of the hatch covers, and so had inspectors and surveyors.

On the *Herald of Free Enterprise*, the owners had focused on productivity, failing to understand the operational challenges of the Zeebrugge ramp and ignoring requests for bow door indicators. The master and crew were under pressure to remain on schedule. They had become complacent about watertight integrity.

On the Estonia, the owners had focused on productivity, failing to value the importance of watertight integrity on a roll-on, roll-off ferry that has high-risk exposure if the bow visor is not designed for the intended purpose. The master and crew were under pressure to remain on schedule, and the master failed to consider the weather and the inadequate bow visor.

On the *Sewol*, the owners had focused on productivity, failing to ensure stability and allowing the ship to sail in an unstable condition. The master and crew had complained, but the owners were not listening, and complacency set in.

On the *El Faro*, the owners had focused on productivity, overlooking the real condition of an old ship. The master headed into the storm rather than selecting an alternate longer route or waiting to let the storm pass. The Coast Guard had failed to conduct proper inspections.

On the Stellar Daisy, the owners were operating an aged converted VLCC operating as a VLOC, the evidence indicates a catastrophic structural failure that led to flooding on the port side.

On a personal note, over my 50 years of work experience, I have also observed the loss of life from accidents. In Canada, I worked for a stevedoring company in the Port of Saint John, New Brunswick. I was the terminal manager at the newly opened forest products export terminal. Stevedoring is the business of loading and unloading ships. Stevedoring companies are hired by either the shipowner or the shipper to undertake the task of handling cargo in and out of ships holds. Every port around the world has stevedoring companies that operate in the ports. They frequently use labor drawn from a pool of workers that are represented by a waterfront union.

In Saint John sometime around 1980, one of the regular shipping lines had their ship alongside the forest product terminal loading rolls of kraft paper. During the loading operation, the terminal delivered the rolls of paper alongside the ship, and the stevedores then placed belt slings around the rolls and lifted them into the ship's hold. The ships were open-hatch type bulk carriers designed for forest products. The open-hatch design allowed the ship's cranes full access to the ships' holds, enabling direct placement. On that afternoon, the rolls of paper slipped out of the belt sling. I do not know the reason—perhaps the sling was defective. The consequence was that the roll fell on top of a stevedore. These rolls weighed two tons each, and he was killed immediately. After this happened, I kept thinking about all the advice that I had received as a cadet: "To never stand under the load," and "To always walk on the non-working side of the deck." These cardinal rules are as valid today as they have always been. I have seen the increasing use of PPE personal protection equipment during my working life, and there is no doubt that High-Viz reflective clothing is excellent at ensuring that people are seen, but this will never substitute for making sure that you are in the right place at the right time. PPE does not make a person immune from harm.

In California, the stevedoring company I managed suffered two fatal accidents, both preventable, and they were "wrong place at the wrong time" situations. The first took place in 1984 during the unloading of steel at night using shore gantry cranes. The foreman was placing steel behind the crane as a buffer stock. The slings from one of the loads failed to clear, and the dockman went to investigate. Insufficient communication between the crane operator and the dockman led to the crane operator hoisting up the sling. The trapped sling tipped the stack of steel and crushed the dockman between the steel and the crane. The dockman suffered fatal injuries. Two years later a clerk working on the terminal was writing down information on a clipboard while large forklifts moved in the same area to load steel onto railcars. The operator of the forklift moves in both directions but is seated facing one, so when proceeding in the other direction the operator must turn to see his route. The forklifts, like all large machinery, are fitted with backup alarms to warn pedestrians of their approach in the operator's visually challenged direction. In this case, the clerk was knocked down by the rear of the forklift, the rear being the steer-axle end. The operator did not see the clerk until the alarm was raised by others who saw the clerk on the ground. Both of these experiences left me with a clear understanding of the inherent risks that exist whenever men and machinery operate together. For the past 30 years, I have drawn from these tragic experiences to positively engage at every place of work, to ensure that all those people who have been influenced by my actions have benefited from what I have learned.

James Reason believes the use of Lost Time Injuries (or "LTI") as a tool for measuring safety is a false indicator, and my own experience concurs with that belief. During my time in the UK steel industry, LTI statistics were a popular benchmark for departments and divisions, with awards for those that reported one-year LTI free. Indicator boards at the entrance to the plant and within each segment reported numbers of days since the last reported LTI. This created a certain amount of stress, because no department wanted to be the one responsible for the LTI board to report that we now had "zero" days since the last LTI. Over time there was a shift towards near-miss reporting, and this is a much more effective approach, but it requires a different collective mindfulness to make it work. Under the LTI system only the incidents that caused lost time were reported, but this ignored the rest of the iceberg, the 90 percent unseen under the water. Like the iceberg, all the mishaps and issues that constitute near-misses simply remained unknown. As a department manager, when I began encouraging near-miss reporting, I knew that this was counter-cultural: nobody wanted to be open about near-misses because this was tantamount to admitting failure or insufficient oversight. I found the first challenge was to ensure that any near-miss reporting was going to be received with a positive response. I knew that near-miss reporting would go underground and remain unknown the moment that anyone was reprimanded because of a near-miss report.

In Chapter Five, I wrote about the panel of inquiry that I co-chaired concerning the overloaded torpedo that derailed, carrying molten iron. Fortunately, there were no injuries, but it was a major near-miss incident. The costs of the repairs and the lost time were significant, in the millions of pounds. This took place around the time near-miss reporting was being introduced as the next step forward in our management of change. I realized that I could send a message to all my team that what happened with the torpedo was a near-miss. I had not seen it coming, and this was a wake-up call to me. I wanted everyone to understand that. I told the story as follows: "The derailed torpedo taught me the following: never assume that just because something is being done a particular way, that this makes it right. I watched those loaded torpedo cars daily from my office window, and I never stopped to ask myself, 'How do we know what they weigh?' A simple question that might have caused us to think differently. So, always apply your mind and ask the right questions." From that time forward, I used my role as the supply chain director to create a positive environment for the team to bring forward near-miss issues. We seized on them as opportunities that needed solutions.

We applied this open approach with our key contractors and, in particular, with the stevedoring company at the port. We encouraged bringing forward near-miss problems so we could find solutions. We held brainstorming sessions so that we could create an open forum for dialog. These led to many collaborative solutions that made the operation safer, eliminating risk, and the best part was everyone had fun being part of it.

In James Reason's 1990 book *Human Error*, Chapter Seven covers "Latent Errors and Systems Disasters." Reason writes, "One of the most remarkable developments of recent years has been the extent to which operators have become increasingly remote from the processes that they nominally control. Machines of growing complexity have come to intervene between the human and the physical task." I am reminded of this when I visit tankers. As a chaplain, I routinely visit the ship's air-conditioned control room with its large windows looking out across the main deck. The control room has large panels with displays, indicator lights, gauges and controls that enable the duty officer to manage the entire flow of oil or liquid from this vantage point. There is no need to venture out on to the deck. This is a process very different to my days on tankers 50 years ago, I was taught the importance of two-valve separation (required to ensure that there was no mixing when different grades of oil are carried) by the physical method of laying hands on the actual valves. When we set up pumping operations, we followed the route and set all the valves needed to create the right flow. The act of opening and closing a valve required significant arm muscle: each main valve required 32 turns to open or close. When these gate valves had to be opened against the pressure of oil in the line, the work needed to close or open increased exponentially with the pressure against the gate valve. There was the pressure of time when loading a tank to the desired 12-inch ullage below the deck (the level of oil in the tank was 12 inches from the top). The valve had to be closed so that the tank did not overfill. This was a two-person operation: while one person closed the valve, another opened the valve to the next tank to be filled. In the past, the operations involved hands-on participation at the sharp end. The current systems are managed from control rooms; this requires a different mindset because a valve is controlled by buttons and switches and the operator relies on remote sensors rather than his own senses.

One area that remains reliant on the senses of the navigating officer is the appreciation of how the ship is managing when working in a storm. The levels of vibration and shuddering as a ship rolls and pitches provide guidance on when to take evasive action. However, to develop these skills requires experience and the ability to interpret the messages that the ship is sending as it works against the power of a storm.

During a winter voyage in the North Atlantic, I was serving as the chief officer on a Canadian bulk carrier headed towards Philadelphia with a cargo of gypsum rock. As we passed east of Nantucket close to the edge of the shallower continental shelf and the deeper waters of the Atlantic, the weather was near storm 10 on the Beaufort scale, and the swells were running deep. The ship was pitching and rolling, shuddering each time that it met the resistance. The captain was on the bridge seated in the pilot chair concentrating on each cycle of the ship's motion and vibration. As the officer of the watch, I became concerned that the southwesterly course that we were maintaining was too much for the sea conditions. The captain had just been promoted to his first command, and he was a good mariner. We had sailed together before. My intuition was that he needed my support and advice. I went over and stood next to the pilot chair and quietly said that I was concerned and suggested that we alter course to ease the strain on the ship. He turned immediately and looked me in the eye and said, "Very good chief—let's do that." We altered course, and the shuddering eased. We soon settled down to a quieter rhythm. The deviation delayed our arrival at the Cape Henlopen pilot by six hours,

224

but better to be six hours late than never to arrive at all. The ship was a belt-type self-unloader with three conveyor belts running the length of our holds. We did not have the benefit of perfect watertight bulkheads. This for me is the true essence of dialog to create change: the opportunity to utilize individual mindfulness to deviate away from potential pathogens.

Eleven: Lessons from the Eight

Each of the eight has its own unique story, and the findings of investigations and inquiries search for answers as to cause and to remedy. What lessons can be learned from a full understanding of what led to each disaster? To determine the lessons, the integrity of the findings is a crucial element. Each disaster involves issues of liability and the desire to assign blame and responsibility. These elements are driven by those who seek to be compensated for a loss and those who seek to defend against such claims. Every disaster will cause a focus on the attribution of liability, and when none can be found or assigned, it may be called a force majeure or an act of God.

The challenge during investigations is to sift through the available data and to discern the reconstruction of events to gain a clear picture of the circumstances that led to the moment when everything went wrong. In the course of the process, there will be some parties who may be reluctant to reveal knowledge for fear this will create liability of themselves or those by whom they are employed. The work of investigators and the task of forensic construction is designed to uncover any blind spots that may be regarded as sensitive and unspoken. The presentation of facts is also essential: members of an adjudicating panel may not have personal experience of all technical matters, and some events can be presented in one way to support a particular argument, but that may not be a correct rendering of what is relevant. The task of attorneys who are defending a client from liability is to cast doubt and introduce alternative theories to divert attention. For this reason, the choice of the person or persons responsible for conducting a maritime investigation is significant. They have the job of establishing the truth. Each flag state has its tradition and custom of how such inquiries take place.

As discussed previously, the United Nations Law of the Sea states that: "Each State shall cause an inquiry to be held by or before a suitably qualified person or persons into every marine casualty or incident of navigation on the high seas involving a ship flying its flag and causing loss of life or serious injury to nationals of another State or serious damage to ships or installations of another State or to the marine environment." The keywords are "to be held by or before a suitably qualified person or persons."

In the United Kingdom, the Department of Transport appoints a wreck commissioner, and they are usually a barrister known as a QC (Queen's Counsel) or a judge. The wreck commissioner can then nominate a team of assessors to provide technical assistance. This method ensures the commissioner is independent and can draw on an impartial panel of experts to assist. Also, because the commissioner is familiar with the workings of the law and legal procedure, they are well versed when dealing with attorneys who represent various interested parties. In the case of the *Derbyshire* and the *Herald of Free Enterprise*, the clarity and depth of insight provided by Justice Colman and Justice Sheen concerning their findings provides a clear understanding of the root causes. In both cases, Justice Colman and Justice Sheen followed the evidence to the root cause without regard to where that might lead. The names of the panel members are published, and each report is signed by them.

In the United States, there is a double track system that has two agencies conducting investigations in parallel. The National Transportation Safety Board and the United States Coast Guard each have their own panel. They collaborate as needed, but they make their own findings and determinations. The Marine Board of Inquiry is a three-person panel appointed by the commandant of the Coast Guard. The panel conducts the investigation and submits a report to the commandant with findings and recommendations. The commandant then reviews the report submitted by the panel and either accepts or rejects the recommendations. The commandant can then put forward separate recommendations and actions. The names of the panel members are published, and each report is signed by them.

We have seen examples in three chapters of the Coast Guard Marine Board of Inquiry process with the *Edmund Fitzgerald, Marine Electric* and the *El Faro*. The challenge evident in all three cases is that, when the panel must evaluate the actions of the Coast Guard itself, this places the panel and the commandant in the difficult situation where they are forced to adjudicate themselves. In the case of the *Edmund Fitzgerald*, the Coast Guard recognized there had been a failure to inspect the system of hatch covers and lifeboat drills properly. On the *Marine Electric*, the Coast Guard inspection system had collapsed leaving no oversight on the condition of the hatch covers. On the *El Faro*, the same inspection system failure detailed in the *Marine Electric* report but not accepted by the commandant was shown to be deficient. The challenge for the Coast Guard is the dilemma of adjudicating themselves when they are a party to the process. They are not an impartial panel, and that raises the question of whether they are "suitably qualified" within the definition of the United Nations Law of the Sea definition. However, the United States has not ratified and joined the Convention now accepted by 162 nations. However, the United States does recognize the Convention as general international law.

The *Estonia* inquiry was jointly conducted by Estonia, Finland, and Sweden. The three nations established a Joint Accident Investigation Commission under an agreement reached between the three prime ministers of each country. The commission was made up of three members from each nation with one of the Estonian members acting as the chairperson. Each nation appointed experts to assist the commission members. The names of the commission members were published.

The report into the loss of the *Sewol* was conducted by the government of South Korea, and the process was affected by the controversy within the government and the disbanding of the Korean Coast Guard following its poor response with the rescue of survivors. In November 2014, the government appointed an independent counsel and 17-member panel. In March 2017, following the election of the new president, Moon Jae-in, a further inquiry was established consisting of an eight-member panel under the chair of Kim Chang-joon. The tireless campaigning efforts of the South Korean people to establish the truth has made a substantial contribution to making sure a legacy of positive change exists.

The report into the loss of the Stellar Daisy has been published without the benefit of the data from the voyage data recorder. They acknowledge receipt of the underwater survey video. However, no reference is made to evidence gained from the footage. The investigation report cannot be considered complete without the benefit of this evidence. The flag state of the ship's registry, the Republic of the Marshall Islands has the responsibility to conduct and deliver the inquiry. Fortunately, the government of South Korea has taken a proactive stance by funding the search for the wreck, the retrieval of the Voyage Data Recorder and an underwater survey. The work by the government of South Korea is in part due to its responsibility as the flag state of the majority of missing seafarers. Also, the campaign by the families of the missing South Korean seafarers has prompted their government to act. Unfortunately, the Marshall Islands maritime administrator is anonymous, we, therefore, do not know the extent of the qualifications held by the person or persons conducting the inquiry. Prior investigation reports published on the IRI website carry no names and no signatures.

Management of change, or change management, is a systematic approach to ensure that there is increased awareness within an organization. This is the work needed to bring about collective mindfulness. Sometimes this is simply known as "joined-up thinking." The Cambridge dictionary defines "joined-up thinking" as: "Thinking about a complicated problem in an intelligent way that includes all the important facts." On each of the ships that are the subject of this book, "Joined up thinking" has been a central part of each story. However, it does not refer only to the actions of the crew responsible for the direct operation of the ship. Charles Perrow, the author of *Normal Accidents*, provides insight into the term "operator error." Perrow writes:

> "Virtually every system we will examine places 'operator error' high on its list of causal factors—generally about 60 to 80 percent of accidents are attributed to this factor. But if, as we shall see time and time again, the operator is confronted by unexpected and usually mysterious interactions among failures, saying that he or she should have zigged instead of zagged is possible only after the fact. Before the accident no one could know what was going on and what should have been done. Sometimes errors are bizarre. We will encounter 'non-collision course collisions,' for example, where ships that were about to pass in the night suddenly turn and ram each other. But careful inquiry suggests that the mariners had quite reasonable explanations for their actions; it is just that the interaction of small failures led them to construct quite erroneous worlds in their minds, and in this case those conflicting images led to collision."

Perrow's book focuses on the issues of the Three Mile Island Nuclear power plant incident near Harrisburg, Pennsylvania, as well as a complete chapter on "Marine

Accidents." In the chapter on "Marine Accidents," Perrow comments about the maritime industry, stating:

> "Much of the marine system is perversely inverted. The identifiable victims are primarily low status, unorganized or poorly organized seamen; the third-party victims of pollution and toxic spills are anonymous, random, and the effects delayed. Elites do not sail on Liberian tankers. The marine courts exist to establish legal liability and settle material claims, not to investigate the cause of accidents and compensate seamen, Shippers do not avoid risky 'bottoms' but pick the cheapest and most convenient and cannot choose to stop shipping for a time because the last cargo was lost. The federal presence is minor and appears inept in the United States; its major impact is to subsidize the shipbuilding and the shipping industry of the US. It sets standards for those ships that want to use our ports, but the United States ranks fourteenth among nations in ship safety, so the standards cannot be very high. And finally, the only international association concerned with safety is advisory and concerned primarily with nationalistic economic goals."

Concerning Perrow's comment (1984) on the ranking of the United States flag for safety, the Paris MoU as of July 2018, shows the United States at the rank of 43rd, placed on the "Grey" list. The Paris MoU website publishes a White, Grey, and Blacklist with data on inspections and detentions.

Perrow's perspective on operator error illustrates the complexity behind the cause of the error or the source of the latent defect. This requires the application of "joined up thinking" when any maritime loss is investigated. We cannot confine our inquiry to the limits of only what took place on board the ship and the behavior of the master and the crew. This is just one part of the story, and might be considered by looking at only the exposed portion of an iceberg. If we apply this to the eight ships covered in this book, we can reveal the unseen part of the iceberg.

On the *Edmund Fitzgerald*, the design of the hatch covers did not provide a workable weathertight system. Most of the time on the Great Lakes, hatch covers were only partially secured. The commercial pressure to maintain a schedule was paramount. The owners and operator's management accepted the above without challenge. The Coast Guard and the classification society responsible for regulatory oversight also accepted it without challenge. After the fact, the Coast Guard admitted the system of hatch covers and their inspection of this was deficient. In the first instance, operator error would be the primary cause, but when we probe further, we find the operators were trapped between a defective design and commercial pressure to maintain schedules.

On the *Derbyshire*, the findings from the Justice Colman inquiry revealed that the design of the hatch covers was inadequate to cope with the weight of green seas. Ventilation pipes on the forecastle were at risk. Although not mentioned in the report, the *Derbyshire* did not have the benefit of a raised forecastle. Freak or abnormal wave heights were known and reported by mariners but were not accepted as fact by naval architects. They were deemed to be "fisherman's tales." The data collected by the Statoil Draupner platform in 1995 revealed the truth about wave behavior. The actions of the Derbyshire Families Association and their 20-year campaign to reveal the truth led to the deployment of underwater technology. This provided answers and paved the way for future use of underwater survey and investigation. The master and crew were not the architects of the *Derbyshire's* design, they were the victims of a failed design.

On the *Marine Electric*, the findings of the Marine Board of Inquiry revealed the failings of the owner's management and the inspection oversight of the Coast Guard and the American Bureau of Shipping. The dedication of Captain Calicchio, the serving panel member with merchant marine experience, to press for change to the inspection regime demonstrated the courage to challenge the system that he was a member of. The *Marine Electric* was a ship operating beyond its useful life. The master and crew kept their commitment, making the shuttle run between Norfolk and Boston in the belief that if anything happened, they would be close to the coast and would be rescued by the Coast Guard. The owners allowed their ship to fall into disrepair, and the Coast Guard and ABS failed to inspect properly. The *Marine Electric* had been converted and also lacked a raised forecastle. The master and crew did not design the *Marine Electric* and they were failed by those who were supposed to serve and protect them.

On the *Herald of Free Enterprise*, the findings from Justice Sheen exposed the "disease of sloppiness" within the corporate culture of the operator's management. The ferry was operating at a terminal in Zeebrugge that required ballasting the ship by the head to access the shore ramps. Masters had requested the fitting of bow door indicators, and higher capacity ballast pumps, only to be denied. The onboard team was under constant pressure to stay on schedule. Operator error caused the bow doors to be left open, but the management failed to provide the additional equipment and did not appreciate the operational challenges faced at Zeebrugge.

On the *Estonia*, the findings of the joint commission revealed the design deficiency of the bow visor. The commercial pressure to remain on schedule resulted in proceeding at full speed during inclement weather across the open Baltic Sea. The master and crew of the *Estonia* were not the designers or builders of the bow visor, they were trapped between a defective design and the commercial pressure of the shuttle service between Tallinn and Stockholm.

On the *Sewol*, the actions of a shipowner who converted the ferry and then caused it to operate in contravention of its stability requirements led to the capsize in broad daylight. The actions of the master and crew to abandon ship without regard to the wellbeing of their passengers is an act that contravenes all maritime tradition. The failure of the South Korean Coastguard to conduct a proactive rescue before the *Sewol* sank, carrying 304 people to their death, is also in contravention of all maritime tradition. The actions of the people of South Korea and the families of the 304 who have campaigned for truth has resulted in the *Sewol* being raised and recovered. The families have demonstrated the power of change by keeping the memory of the 304 alive.

Regarding the *El Faro*, the Marine Board of Inquiry revealed that the 40-year-old *El Faro* was likely operating with serious defects that the Coast Guard and the American Bureau of Shipping had failed to inspect properly. Following the *El Faro* loss, the Coast Guard inspected the sister vessel *El Yunque* and found serious defects that led to the *El Yunque* being withdrawn from service and scrapped. The *El Faro* and *El Yunque* were both employed on a regular shuttle service between Jacksonville, Florida and San Juan, Puerto Rico. The *El*

Faro had been converted for this trade, carrying containers on deck, which altered the stability and resulted in a tender condition. The low freeboard placed the hold ventilation scuttles close to the waterline, but these were routinely left open. A decision by Captain Davidson to take the shortest route led to a voyage that collided with Hurricane Joaquim. The effects of windage on the deck containers led to a starboard list and cargo breaking free, which in turn led to flooding of the holds. The starboard list was corrected by turning the ship against the wind, and because of her tender condition, the list reversed to a port list. However, the port list had the adverse effect of losing all main propulsion when the steam turbines lost suction of the lubricating oil in the sump. The *El Faro* succumbed to the beam seas, flooding and rapidly sinking. Captain Davidson was under commercial pressure to stay on schedule and he was vying for a position on a newly constructed vessel. The findings of the Marine Board of Inquiry once again raised the same problem of quality of Coast Guard inspections and the use of third-party inspectors. Similar recommendations made after the *Marine Electric* but subsequently rejected by the commandant. The master and crew of the *El Faro* did not design the conversion. Like the *Marine Electric*, they were failed by those who were supposed to serve and protect them.

The wreck of the Stellar Daisy has now been located, and the voyage data recorder recovered. The formal inquiry by the flag state has been issued. Fortunately, there is evidence from the two survivors, and this provides additional insight to the events leading up to the moment that the Stellar Daisy rolled on her port side and sank. The Republic of the Marshall Islands and the office of the Maritime Administrator are in charge of the inquiry. This work is contracted to a US based company called International Registries, Inc "IRI." The identity of the person or persons that comprise the Maritime Administrator is anonymous, and therefore it is difficult to assess whether they are suitably qualified as required under the United Nations Convention on the law of the sea "UNCLOS."

The unseen part of the iceberg, the common thread that appears in all cases (except for the *Stellar Daisy* where the inquiry is awaited) are design issues. Four of the eight ships had been subject to significant conversions, which clearly had a notable effect on their operation. The *Stellar Daisy* was also a conversion. There is a need for more "joined up thinking" when shipowners call for designs from naval architects and shipbuilders. Engagement with the professionals who will be called on to operate the ship would lead to positive dialogue and collaboration.

The recent incident involving the cruise ship *Viking Sky* off the Norwegian coast provides a chilling near-miss that could have resulted in a major loss of life. The loss of all electrical power during an intense storm has been attributed to the four diesel engines shutting down automatically due to a loss of lubricating oil pressure. Reports from the Norwegian safety authorities suggest that the motion of the ship in the storm caused a loss of suction in the sump tanks. The tanks contained a reduced level of oil at the time of the incident. (This is the same fault suffered by the *El Faro*.) The *Viking Sky* was designed as an all-electric ship, so the loss of electrical power shut down propulsion as well as all auxiliaries. The *Viking Sky* was then vulnerable to the force of the storm. The *Viking Sky* declared an emergency and the Norwegian Coast Guard began a mammoth airlift by helicopter, with almost 500 people taken ashore. However, that left 873 remaining onboard. This illustrates the limited ability and complexity to airlift large numbers of people in a short timeframe. The *Viking Sky* is a relatively small cruise ship compared to the mega-cruise liners sailing today. Also of note is the number of enclosed lifeboats fitted. Only three can be seen on the port side in the photos of the ship entering the port of Molde. The *Viking Sky* incident raises questions: Why did the design and build of the oil sumps not consider the effect of severe weather? Why did all four engines shut down? Did the design make provision for emergency power? Why were they sailing in that area during a major storm? Why do cruise ships accept passengers who may be physically unable to cope with a rescue at sea? Finally, as the *Viking Sky* approached the rocks, would it have been possible to evacuate the passengers via lifeboats and life-rafts under such conditions?

Looking at two major non-maritime incidents that are currently under inquiry, we can also learn something from the process. On June 14, 2017, in London, the 24-story Grenfell Tower block of flats caught fire in the early hours of the morning, killing 72 people. This is the worst peacetime residential fire ever to have occurred in the United Kingdom, burning for 60 hours with graphic video footage carried around the world by the television networks. The fire led to a massive emergency response from the London Fire Brigade and other emergency services. The Grenfell public inquiry began on September 14, 2017. The rapid spread of the fire has been attributed to the system of cladding retrofitted to the exterior of the tower block. Prime Minister Theresa May announced a public inquiry and appointed Sir Martin Moore-Bick, a retired appeals court judge, to preside over it. The inquiry expects to commence phase two in 2020, illustrating the time needed to explore all the facts fully. In a December 9, 2018, report by the *Guardian* newspaper, Tim Adams provides a recap of the first phase of the trial.

> "When very bad things happen, those directly involved would sit somewhere like this, 18 months or two years down the line, in front of a polite QC and a retired judge and a bank of lawyers with box files, and try, often in vain, over the course of an afternoon, to knot their brows and recall their part in the tragic events in question… The Grenfell inquiry is now six

months into a process that is expected to last two more years. Next week, phase one of its remit, which has gathered documentary evidence and interrogated core participants over statements about the events of the night itself, will come to an end. The presiding chair, Sir Martin Moore-Bick, will publish a preliminary report, which may lead to some immediate statutory changes, for example in building regulations relating to cladding, and in updated guidance to firefighters dealing with high-rise fires…"

"The public inquiry—first used as an instrument for the Tay Bridge Disaster, which killed 75 people in 1879 [it found that the bridge had been 'badly designed, badly built and badly maintained,' though no prosecutions followed]—is one of Britain's genuine growth industries."

One of the key areas under review by the inquiry is the London Fire Brigade's use of the "stay-put" policy in place before Grenfell. The theory on which this was based was that, in a tower block fire, the residents were safer to "stay-put" rather than to evacuate. The "stay-put" order was changed to evacuate within two hours of the fire starting. The consequences of the "stay-put" order will be covered by Moore-Bick. The "stay-put" instruction is reminiscent of the instructions given to the passengers—mostly high school students on the *Sewol* ferry.

The appointment of a retired judge to lead the Grenfell inquiry is intended to provide an independent adjudication of the facts by a person who is trained in the law. When the United Nations Convention on the Law of the Sea stipulated that "Each State shall cause an inquiry to be held by or before a suitably qualified person or persons," the definition of suitably qualified should mean a person knowledgable in matters of law and independent. For example, the British public would not accept the London Fire Brigade to be responsible for conducting an inquiry into the Grenfell fire. However, when we compare this to the system of Marine Board of Inquiry in the United States, we find that the Coast Guard is in charge of conducting the inquiry even though, as the agency responsible for oversight of maritime law, as well as search and rescue, it is a party of interest in its own investigations.

Another example of this biased approach has been revealed in the investigations underway into the accidents of two Boeing 737 Max 8 aircraft in Indonesia on October 29, 2018, and Ethiopia on March 10, 2019. In both cases, there were no survivors. This has led to the global grounding of the Boeing 737 Max 8 fleet on March 13, 2019. In an article published in the *New Yorker* magazine on March 18, 2019, John Cassidy revealed the following:

> "Boeing has promised a software fix to address some of the potential problems created by the MCAS. That's too little, too late, of course,

and it doesn't address the even larger issue of how the 737 Max was allowed to fly in the first place. On Sunday, the *Seattle Times*, the home-town newspaper of Boeing's commercial division, published the results of a lengthy investigation into the federal certification of the 737 Max. It found that the FAA outsourced key elements of the certification process to Boeing itself, and that Boeing's safety analysis of the new plane contained some serious flaws, including several relating to the MCAS."

Cassidy went on to pose the following critical question: "How can a manufacturer of something as complex and potentially dangerous as a passenger jet be allowed to play such a large role in deciding whether its product is safe? It turns out that the FAA, with congressional approval, has 'over the years delegated increasing authority to Boeing to take on more of the work of certifying the safety of its own airplanes,' the *Seattle Times* said. In the case of the 737 Max, which is a longer and more fuel-efficient version of previous 737s, Boeing was particularly eager to get the plane into service quickly, so it could compete with Airbus's new A320neo."

The loss of the two aircraft has now revealed a truly startling fact: the Federal Aviation Agency had allowed an aircraft manufacturer to self-certify.

In the case of the maritime industry, the certification process is governed by independent Classification Societies. The report into the loss of the Estonia explained their function in great detail. They stated:

"The first classification society was formed in the mid-18th century to give underwriters independent information about the condition of ships intended to be insured. Several other classification societies were formed at the beginning of the nineteenth century. The main purpose of a classification society is to perform neutral surveys and inspections. A classification society is engaged for a given ship by the shipowner from the design stage of the new building, through the construction phase and subsequently throughout the life of the ship. A classification, carried out by a recognised society, is normally a requirement of insurance companies... Classification societies are generally organised as non- profit organisations and charge shipyards and shipowners for their services at cost."

To understand the path of commercial interests a rule of thumb is to "follow the money."

Classification societies receive their revenue from the shipowners and shipbuilders, and this has the potential to create a bias in favor of the source of the income. Some

50 classification societies are operating around the world. The 13 largest belong to the International Association of classification societies ("IACS") founded in Hamburg, Germany in 1968. IACS has consultative status at the International Maritime Organization ("IMO").

Classification societies issue certificates in exchange for fees. Classification societies compete for the business of serving shipowners, and some shipowners will make a change if they believe they can find more favorable conditions for their ships.
In the case of the eight ships reviewed in this book, we have seen many instances of the failure of classification societies to conduct proper inspections. All three of the ships served by the American Bureau of Shipping experienced insufficient diligence by the society surveyors. In the case of the *Derbyshire*, the hatch covers were built to the rules of Lloyd's Register, and these rules were found to be inadequate. The conversion of the *Sewol* was the subject of scrutiny with the Korean Register, and the *Stellar Daisy* conversion was also overseen by the Korean Register. For the maritime industry to be safe, the system of oversight must act without bias or influence. This means that the classification societies have to assert themselves even when this means insisting on actions that may cause conflict with the commercial interests of their client.

Throughout all the of the eight, there is a recurring fact that knowledge was not shared, the right dialog did not take place. Information was kept in discreet pockets to suit the agenda of those who held the authority. Cultures that contain these deficiencies are vulnerable to failure. Professor James Reason highlights this in his book *A Life in Error*. Reason deals with the issue of "Cultural Strata" and cites the work of Patrick Hudson. Hudson who described five cultures of safety management.

• Pathological	Blame, denial and the blinkered pursuit of excellence. Financial targets prevail: cheaper/faster.
• Reactive	Safety given attention after an event, there is concern about adverse publicity. The organization establishes an incident reporting system.
• Bureaucratic	There are systems in place to manage safety, often in response to external pressures. Data harvested rather than analyzed and used. Safety management is strictly by the book.
• Proactive	Aware that "Latent pathogens" and "error traps" lurk within the system. Seek to eliminate them before they combine to cause an accident. Management listens to experts and "sharp-enders."
• Generative	Respects, anticipates and responds to risks. A just, learning, flexible, adaptive, prepared and informed culture. Strives for resilience.

The outcome of the eight may well have been different had the culture been of the "Proactive" and "Generative" level. Culture is not limited to those who operated the ships. This has broad scope and includes everyone from design and build to those who had oversight and the authority to control.

The signs exist, and they are the clues to the pathogens or latent defects that are embedded in almost every ship as they are in virtually every system. The challenge is how to behave with an enhanced awareness to recognize the warning signs and to know how to act and when to act. This requires the courage of Calicchio, to never succumb to commercial pressure. This means finding the right dialog with colleagues that creates a collaborative space ensuring that you never have to pass through that final hole in the Swiss Cheese Model.

"I have often marveled at the thin line which separates success from failure" –
Sir Ernest Shackleton

Bibliography

Aristoi Academy. *Edmund Fitzgerald.* https://www.aristoiclassical.org/apps/video/watc h.jsp?v=88217

BBC. *Horizon BBC Freak Waves.* https://www.youtube.com/watch?v=mC8bHxgd HH4. 2002.

BBC. *Vale the pride of Brazil becomes its most hated company.* https://www.bbc.com/news/business-47056849. 2019.

BBC. *Grenfell Tower: Why was "stay put" advice so disastrous.* https://www.bbc.com/news/uk-44360696#. 2018.

BBC. *Viking Sky: Engine failure blamed on low oil levels.* https://www.bbc.com/news/world-europe-47727267. 2019.

BIMCO. *Port State Control Inspections in the USA.* http://www.bimco.dk/upload/us_psci_folder_hig h.pdf_. 2006.

Cool Merchant Mariners. *Stellar Daisy* Survivors. https://www.facebook.com/coolmariners/?hc_ref =ARQqHXzsoQKGBiOJSqe-Grv15z23PQZMmvtf_CnzBuvull3vRKJt8RDl-Bee_Ehh1K8&__xts__%5B0%5D=68.ARATo7 PlwQx3own5O31zMPpNUn0D97-m8ts-biSjzJyDTEU92lJHS2rsLh-

fwQ7vC1Wj4DpnPPvBDsoKii0VZ72VzMjHsP
hONyKp19tOOT5_xg54mmnEToLOkHKHwlyc
WH17clXmcDXrTuwpH14nkwOXMFzpnXf7IB
MglhxmK1H3L-
lIO_C6OuLvBHpQWSo08nQt5D030wR_wGaFf
7eh7ibWxDki5-1CbGzcmoUKtNIZiVTeb-
Plb3j8ctzyiNM7VQsrL_Au7xvhNY41hzdf-
U_BUwPnRBste9A62te4qPajb0XtnLhSeN0fzJg
nDnmFY341fqnOtk0n6iPlOr0MPexDqQ&__tn_
_=kC-R. 2017.

Department of Transport. *Herald of Free Enterprise –
Formal Investigation.*
https://assets.publishing.service.gov.uk/media/54
c1704ce5274a15b6000025/FormalInvestigation_
HeraldofFreeEnterprise-MSA1894.pdf. 2015

Devanney, J. *The Strange History of Tank Inerting.*
www.c4tx.org/ctx/pub/igs.pdf. 2005.

Edwards, B. *Return of the Coffin Ships.* New York:
Bricktower Press. 1998.

Estonia. *Report of the Commission of Inquiry.*
http://onse.fi/estonia/brindex.html. 1997.

Faulkner, D. *Rogue Waves—Defining Their
Characteristics for Marine Design.*
http://www.ifremer.fr/web-
com/molagnon/bv/Faulkner_w.pdf. 2000.

Foy, G. M. *Run the Storm.* New York: Scribner. 2018.

Frump, R. *Until the Sea Shall Free Them.* New York:
Doubleday. 2002

Frump, R. *The Captains of Thor*. Middletown, DE: Frump. 2018

Kwon, Yisug. *System Theoretic Safety Analysis of the Sewol-Ho Ferry Accident in South Korea*. http://sunnyday.mit.edu/papers/Kwon-Thesis.pdf. 2016.

Leveson, N. G. *Engineering a Safer World*. Cambridge MA: MIT Press. 2011.

Lloyd's Register. *Carrying solid bulk cargoes safely*. https://www.ukpandi.com/fileadmin/uploads/ukpi/Documents/Events/2016/IMSBC_Carrying_S olid_Bulk_cargoes_safely_in_the_properties201 6.pdf. 2016

Marine Accident Investigation Branch. *Braer*. https://www.gov.uk/maib-reports/engine-failure-and-subsequent-grounding-of-oil-tanker-braer-at-garths-ness-shetland-scotland. 1993.

Morrell, M. & Capparell, S. *Shackleton's Way*. London: Nicholas Brealey. 2001.

North of England P&I. *Iron Ore Fines*. http://www.nepia.com/media/647929/LP-Briefing-Iron-Ore-Fines-March-2017.PDF . 2017.

Perrow, C. *Normal Accidents*. Princeton, NJ: Princeton University. 1984.

Ramsay, R. *For Whom the Bell Tolls*. Pittsburgh, PA: Dorrance. 2006.

Ramwell, D. & Madge, T. *A Ship Too Far*. London: Hodder & Stoughton. 1992.

Reason, J. *A Life in Error*. Burlington, VT: Ashgate. 2013

Reason, J. *Organizational Accidents Revisited*. Boca Raton, FL: CRC Press. 2016.

Reason, J. *Human Error*. Cambridge: Cambridge University Press. 1990.

Royal Institute of Naval Architects. *Lessons must be learned from ore carrier sinking*. 2017

Schumacher, M. *Mighty Fitz*. Minneapolis, MN: Bloomsbury. 2005.

Spiegel Online. *Scientists Unveil Cause of Estonia Ferry Disaster*.
http://www.spiegel.de/international/europe/simul ating-a-fatal-turn-scientists-unveil-cause-of-estonia-ferry-disaster-a-527875.html. 2008.

Stutz, B. *Rogue Waves,*
http://discovermagazine.com/2004/jul/rogue-waves. July 25, 2004

Tankershipping.com. *Mobile Inert Gas Systems*.
https://www.tankershipping.com/news/view,the-evolution-of-mobile-inert-gas-systems-in-the-tanker-trade_42742.htm. 2016

Tasca, L. *The Social Construction of Human Error.* Thesis (Ph.D.). State University of New York. 1990.

US Chemical Safety and Hazard Investigation Board. Investigation Report BP Texas City. https://www.csb.gov/bp-america-refinery-explosion/. 2007.

US Coast Guard. *Compass Blog. Marine Electric.* http://coastguard.dodlive.mil/2014/08/lessons-from-30-year-old-disaster-still-saving-lives-today/. 2014.

US Coast Guard. *Compass Blog: The Long Blue Line: Domenic Calicchio.* https://coastguard.dodlive.mil/2016/02/the-long-blue-line-domenic-calicchio-champion-of-marine-safety-regulations/. 2016.

US DOT. *Marine Casualty Report: Marine Electric.* https://www.dco.uscg.mil/Portals/9/DCO%20Do cuments/5p/CG-5PC/INV/docs/boards/marineelectric.pdf. Jan 1985.

US DOT. *Marine Casualty Report: El Faro.* https://media.defense.gov/2017/Oct/01/20018201 87/-1/-1/0/FINAL%20PDF%20ROI%2024%20SEP%2 017.PDF. 2017

Wilson, D. *The Hole.* UK: Exposure. 2006.

YouTube. *Sinking of the Derbyshire.*
https://www.youtube.com/watch?v=9tN4xROtM
jI. 2011

Acknowledgments

My inspiration to write this book came from meeting the Philadelphia SESAMO group, the Korean-American group who are part of the global awareness campaign created to remember the loss of the 304 lives on the ferry *Sewol*.

This book would not have been possible without the constant support and encouragement of my wife and life partner Ann. When I had doubts, she gave me the courage to press on and helped me find my voice.

Special thanks to the three colleagues who gave me steady encouragement as I wrote the chapters: Andrew Himmel, Eugene Mattioni and Trevor Wilkinson.

My career in the shipping industry began in November of 1968. I have had the benefit of experiencing a wide variety of activity both at sea and ashore. Over 50 years I had the privilege of being mentored and guided by individuals who shared their knowledge with me. My journey has been rich with exposure to the world of; seafaring, stevedoring, terminal operations, chartering, ship operation, port operations, supply chain management, steel works management and transportation consulting. This has given me a unique lens as an observer. I owe a debt of gratitude to all of the people that I journeyed with—our dialog kept us safe.

In the twilight of my career, I have trained to serve as a chaplain volunteering my time to work in hospice, hospitals and with my local seafarer center. The services provided by all seafarer centers make a significant contribution to the wellbeing of all seafarers, and I encourage you to support their work.

Glossary of Terms

ABS:	American Bureau of Shipping, a classification society.
ACP:	USCG—Alternative Compliance Program.
ACS:	USCG—Approved classification society.
Articles:	Ship's document for seafarers to sign on or off, a contract of agreement.
Beaufort scale:	A scale of wind speed based on observation from Force 0 to Force 12 named after Sir Francis Beaufort.
Bilges:	Drainage compartment in a ship's hold.
Bow:	The forward end of a ship.
Bulk Carrier:	Ship designed for the carriage of dry cargo in bulk.
Bulkhead:	Partition between two spaces.
Bulwarks:	A solid extension of the ships side above the level of the main deck.
Bunkers:	Fuel to provide power to main engines and auxiliary power.
Camouflage:	To blend with the surroundings.
Cape-Size:	Ship too wide to transit the Suez Canal.
CCTV:	Closed Circuit Television.
CEO:	Chief Executive Officer.
Charterer:	Company that hires a ship either on a time or voyage basis.
Charter Party:	The agreement between a shipowner and a charterer for the use of the ship.

Cleats:	On a ship, the securing clamps to hold the hatch cover to the coaming.
CNN:	Cable Network News.
Coaming:	Vertical plating surrounding a hatch opening that supports the hatch covers.
Commandant:	Leader of the United States Coast Guard.
Davits:	Mechanism for the launch of lifeboats by gravity.
Deadweight:	Ship's carrying capacity of cargo, stores, bunkers, water and provisions.
DOC:	Document of Compliance.
Double Bottom:	The space underneath the ship's cargo hold and the hull, used as a tank to carry bunkers or water ballast.
Draft:	The measurement of a ship's submerged depth, measured forward, aft and midships on both sides.
Ferry:	Ship used to transport cargo or passengers over short distances on a regular schedule.
Forecastle:	The raised foredeck area.
Freeboard:	Distance from the main deck to the waterline.
GM:	Metacentric height, measure of restoring force.
Great Circle:	The shortest navigational distance. A curved line on a Mercator chart.
Highway Code:	UK guide and mandatory rules for all road users.

Hi-Viz:	Clothing either in Lime green or Orange with reflective stripes.
Hurricane:	See Typhoon.
INTERCARGO:	International Association of Dry Cargo Shipowners.
ITF:	International Transport workers Federation.
Jones Act:	US Merchant Marine Act of 1920, section 27.
Kestner:	A patented clamp device used on Great Lakes vessels to secure hatch lids.
Knot:	One nautical mile per hour.
KR:	Korean Register of Shipping, a classification society.
Lakers:	Ships designed for trading within the Great Lakes and Rivers system.
Liquefaction:	Solid that is water-saturated and is transformed into a slurry.
Lloyd's:	Lloyd's Register of Shipping, a classification society.
LO-LO:	Lift-on–lift-off, referring to cargo handled by cranes not driven onboard.
LORACS:	USCG—List of Recognized and Authorized classification societies.
MARAD:	US Maritime Administration.
MBI:	Marine Board of Inquiry (US).
MISLE:	USCG—Marine Information for Safety and Law Enforcement.
Nautical Mile:	6080 feet.
NTSB:	National Transportation Safety Board (US).
OBO:	Ore-Bulk-Oil Carrier
OCMI:	USCG—Officer in Charge Maritime Investigation.

Panamax:	A ship narrow enough to pass through the original Panama Canal.
PandI:	Insurance company providing Protection and Indemnity insurance to shipowners and charterers.
Paris MoU:	Port State Control operated by 27 cooperating nations.
Plimsoll:	The circular mark displayed midships on each side of a ship that signifies the maximum submergence permissible on summer load lines. Named after Samuel Plimsoll.
PPE:	Personal Protective Clothing.
Rhumb Line:	Navigational course which passes all meridians at the same angle, a straight line on a Mercator chart.
RMI:	Republic of the Marshall Islands.
Salties:	Term used by Lakers to describe ocean-hopping ships that travel within the Great Lakes network.
Self-Unloader:	A ship capable of unloading its cargo with shipboard equipment.
SESAMO:	South Korean—People in Solidarity with the Families of the *Sewol* Ferry.
Scantlings:	Dimensions and standards for ship construction approved by classification societies.
Stevedore:	The workers employed to load and unload ships at a port.
Stiff:	Condition of ship stability when the GM is larger and roll period is short. Opposite of Tender.

Swell:	Motion of the sea due to the effect of storms.
Taconite:	A form of iron ore mined in Minnesota, US.
Tank-top:	The steel floor of a cargo hold.
Tender:	Condition of ship stability when the GM is smaller and roll period is long. Opposite of Stiff.
Ton:	Metric weight measure equal to 1000 kilos or approximately 2204.6 pounds.
Typhoon:	The term for a rotational cyclone that develops in the Northern hemisphere over the Pacific Ocean. Equivalent to a hurricane in the Atlantic or a cyclone in the South Pacific or Indian Ocean.
T2:	World War II standard design Tanker steam turbine generator with electric propulsion.
USCG:	United States Coast Guard.
VDR:	Voyage data recorder.
VLCC:	Very Large Crude Carrier
VLOC:	Very Large Ore Carrier
Wedges:	Fastening devices used to secure sections of hatch covers when closed.
Windlass:	Ships's mooring winch on forecastle used to raise anchors and handle mooring ropes.

Index

A

A Life in Error	86, 124, 248
Abnormal waves	45, 215
Admiral Gracey	158, 159,161,162
Admiral Lusk	161
Alexandre P	44
Algarrobo	44
American Bureau of Shipping	65, 77, 78, 153, 158, 159, 160, 161, 236, 238, 247
Andrew Rajner	24
Angle of loll	133
Antarctic	2, 6
Aristoi Academy	25
Arthur M. Anderson	26, 27

B

Barranger	72, 73
Bay of Biscay	47, 103
Bencruachan	45, 48
Bilges	43, 65, 192, 195, 196, 201, 202, 203, 204, 211, 212
BISCO Ore Carrier Fleet	40
Bob Cusick	64, 65, 72, 73, 75, 76
Bob Frump	71, 159
Boeing	244, 245, 246
Bolshevik Revolution	128
Bolshoi Theatre	129
Bow door	13, 81, 87, 103, 104, 107, 108, 109, 113, 122, 216, 237
BP	97, 98, 99, 114, 122
Braer	117, 118, 122, 123
British India Steam Navigation	126
British Shipping Federation	9
British Steel	37, 40, 62
Brittany	60, 121, 173
Brumadinho	75, 196
Bureau Veritas	106, 107

C

C. S. Loosmore 27
Cabot Strait 69, 70
Cabotage 147, 148, 150, 160, 161, 171, 175
Calicchio 77, 78, 79, 156, 159, 160, 161, 162, 163, 165,171, 172, 175, 236, 249
Canadian Century 22
Canadian Ranger 18
Canadian Transport 39, 190
Cape Henlopen 224
Captain David Lewry 80
Captain Davidson 24, 174, 238, 239
Captain Farnham 65
Captain Kirby 88
Captain Lauridsen 162
Captain Lee Jun-seok 139
Captain McSorley 24, 29, 33, 34, 215
Captain Underhill 42, 215
Captain Zabinski 29
Carl Burgner 28
Carlton 67
Challenger 121
Change management 231
Choi Duk-ha 125
Chonghaejin Marine 132, 139, 140
Classification Societies 106, 189, 246, 247, 248
Clinometer 48, 208
Coast Guard 25, 28, 29, 32, 33, 65, 72-75, 77, 78, 116, 118, 125, 138, 144, 145, 151-166, 169-171, 173-175, 217, 228-230, 235, 236, 238, 239, 241, 244
Coffin ships 7, 115, 116, 192
Colin Armitage 72, 74
Collective mindfulness 89, 90, 92, 102, 104, 171, 214, 220, 231
COMAH 102
Commandant Gracey 163, 165, 175
Complacency 8, 14, 27, 31, 34, 137, 146, 216
Corporate Manslaughter and Homicide act in 2007 81, 82
Corus 37, 81-84, 93, 94, 100, 102, 213
Crowley Maritime 174
Cyclone Fifi 44

D

Dampier 44
Daniel Ludwig 39, 40
Danwon High School 124, 125, 130, 131, 140, 143, 145, 146
Deepwater Horizon 98, 179
Department of Homeland Security 160
Department of Transport 55, 67, 148, 227
Deputy Prime Minister John Prescott 56
Derbyshire 12, 20, 36, 41-44, 46, 47, 53-56, 58-62,64, 66, 116, 138, 185, 192, 197, 199, 215, 228, 235, 236, 248
Dewey 73, 74
Discovery 4, 52
Disease of sloppiness 86, 146, 174, 236
DOC 166-168, 170
Dockwise White Marlin 142
Dorchester 143, 144
Douglas Faulkner 58
Draupner 46, 52-54, 235
DuPont 117

E

Edmund Fitzgerald 6, 13-15, 17, 18, 22, 23, 25, 29, 32-34, 70, 71, 199, 214, 215, 229, 234
El Faro 13, 24, 42, 71, 78, 147-150, 152, 153, 155, 160, 163, 165, 166, 170, 171, 174, 175, 188, 199, 205, 211, 214, 216, 229, 238, 239, 241
El Morro 148, 170
El Yunque 148, 152, 165-170, 205, 238
Elephant Island 7
Elpida 176
Endurance 2-4, 6
Erica 60
Esso 117, 213
Estline 105, 122
Estonia 13, 105-109, 113, 114, 118, 122, 123, 131, 199, 216, 230, 237, 246
Eugene Kelly 73
Exxon Valdez 116

F

Ferry Naminoue 132
Final Inquiry 41, 108, 109
Finnamore Meadow 62, 66
Finnish Maritime Administration 106
Flushing Range 103
For Whom the Bell Tolls 20, 35
Four Chaplains 143, 144
Francesco Fedele 52
Freak wave 45, 52, 58, 61

G

Georgia Institute of Technology 52
Gerald Darling 55
Global Infinity 176, 177, 198
Google Earth 46
Graham Danton 48, 49
Grenfell 75, 117, 242-244
Gulf of St Lawrence 15, 69, 110
Gulf Stream 69, 120
Gwanghwamun Square 141
Gwangju District court 139

H

Han Yun-ji 143
Haverton Hill 37
Health and Safety Executive 83
Herald of Free Enterprise 13, 31, 80, 81, 85, 86, 103-105, 108, 109, 113, 116, 131, 146, 215, 216, 228, 236
Highway Code 95-97
Hilda Marjanne 18, 19, 22
Huasco 45
Human Error 150, 222
Hurricane Joaquim 78, 149, 175, 238

I

IFREMER 58, 59
Ilha Guaiba 202

IMO	179, 181, 185, 247
Incheon	124, 132, 135
Individual mindfulness	89, 90, 92, 123, 171, 213, 214, 225
Inert gas systems	114, 115
INTERCARGO	186-188
International Registries, Inc.	178, 240
IRI	178-181, 231, 240
ISMBC	191
ITF	55

J

Jeju	124, 125, 130, 143
Jim McCann	73
Jindo Island	12, 145, 183
John Betjeman	8
Joined up thinking	232, 234, 240
Jos L. Meyer	105
Journal of Marine Structures	58
Jung Hon-Won	139
Justice Colman	41, 53, 56, 57, 228, 235
Justice Sheen	80, 81, 86, 88, 95, 102, 104, 113, 146, 174, 228, 236

K

Kang Min-kyu	140
Kawasaki	36, 45
Ken Cooke	74
Kestner	20, 21, 25, 27, 28, 30, 34
Kevin Downey	84
Kong Haakon VII	114, 115
Korean Register of Shipping	132, 140, 183, 205, 211
Korean Shipping Association	139
Kure shipyard	39, 40
Kwon Hyeok-gyu	167
Kwon Jae-geun	143
Kwon Ji-yeon	143

L

Lake Superior	13, 15, 19, 21, 23, 26, 70, 71
Lakers	15, 17-19, 26, 27, 30

Latent defects   2, 24, 29, 33-35, 61, 71, 75, 76, 81, 85, 94, 109, 117, 145, 149, 175, 205, 210, 212, 214, 249

Laurentian Trough   69

Leslie Sabel   80, 81

Lids   20, 23, 30, 101

Linear model of wave analysis   45

Liquefaction   186-188, 191-193, 196, 197, 201, 206, 207

Lisolette Fredette   78

Liverpool Bridge   42

Lloyd's   5, 7, 190, 248

London and Overseas Freighters   10

London Citizen   16, 17

London Fire Brigade   242-244

London Prestige   11, 42

London Statesman   45, 47, 49, 51

Lord Donaldson   41, 55, 58

LTI   220

Lulworth Hill   72

M

MacGregor   19, 21

Mactra   114, 115

Maenggol Channel   124, 131

Marine Board of inquiry   25-29, 31, 64, 65, 76, 77, 149, 152, 156, 157, 159, 160, 163, 165, 171, 175, 228, 229, 236, 238, 239, 244

Marine Electric   13, 14, 20, 31, 42, 62, 64-66, 67, 71, 72, 74, 76-78, 116, 150, 151, 156, 157, 159, 160, 162, 163, 175, 185, 188, 198, 211, 214, 215, 229, 236, 239

Marine Transport Lines   65, 74, 77

Maritime Administrator   179-181, 198, 200, 201, 204, 205, 209, 210, 231, 239, 240

Mark Victor Stanley   80

Marpessa   114, 115

Marshall Islands 137, 177-181, 198-200, 203, 205, 210, 211, 231, 239

Martin Moore-Bick   242, 243

MCAS   245

Merchant Navy   8, 9, 11

Metacentric height or "GM,"   38, 132

Michael Schumacher   24

Mineral Diamond   44

Mokpo   142

Moon Jae-in   141, 230

N

Navy Yard   144
Neo-Confucian   130
Nevasa   126-128, 130, 131
New Yorker   245
Nordstrom and Thulin   122
Normal Accidents   150, 232
Not Under Command   111, 120
NTSB   28, 29, 32, 151

O

OBO's (Ore-Bulk-Oil carrier)   37, 44, 185
Occupational Safety   85
Ocean-routes   56-58
Ontario Power   109-112
Ore Transport   39
Organizational Accidents Revisited   89, 213
Orinoco River   40, 120

P

P&O European Ferries   103
Panamax bulk carrier   40, 119
PandI   184
Paris MoU   173, 234
Park Geun-Hye   139, 141
Pasithea   44
Pathogens   33, 35, 145, 225, 249
Philadelphia Inquirer   159, 162
Philippe Varin   82, 93
Phosphore Conveyor   90, 119, 121, 191
Plimsoll   7, 78, 115, 116, 132, 133
Plymouth College   48
Poet   78, 150, 151
Polaris   177, 183, 186, 201, 204, 211
Port of Saint John   36, 217
Port State Control   173, 174
Port Talbot   82-85, 93

PPE   218
Process Safety   82, 85, 95, 97, 98, 117
Professor James Reason   1, 2, 3,86, 89, 248
Prudhoe Bay oil spill   97

Q

QC   227, 242

R

Raymond Ramsay   20, 35
Redcar Steelworks   37
Return of the Coffin Ships   192
Richard Rogers   5
Risk management   117
Robert Falcon Scott   4
Robert Frump   12, 65, 71, 76, 78
Rogue Waves — Defining Their Characteristics for Marine Design 58
Royal Institute of Naval Architects   186

S

Saltie   15, 17, 18, 20, 26
Schichau Unterweser shipyard   105
SCI   135, 136
Scunthorpe   36
Seabed Constructor   176
Seamen's Church Institute   71, 134, 126
Seattle Times   245, 246
Sept Iles   36, 110, 173, 192
SESAMO (People in Solidarity with the Families of the *Sewol* Ferry)
     126, 134, 137, 138, 257
Sewol   12, 13, 17, 124-126, 130-142, 145, 146, 183, 188, 214, 216,
     230, 237, 238, 244, 248, 257
Shanghai Salvage Company   141
Shell Tankers   114
Short Brothers   67
Sinter Fines   197
Sir Ernest Shackleton   2, 250
Smit-Tak Towage and Salvage   103
SOLAS   107

Sorel   40
South Georgia   4
South Korean Ministry of Oceans and Fisheries   139
Southgate Technical college   8
Spirit class   88-90, 105
St Lawrence Prospector   21, 66, 67, 75
Static electricity   115, 122
Statoil   46, 52, 235
Steamship Mutual   184, 185
Stellar Daisy 6, 137, 138, 176, 177, 183, 186, 188, 189, 198-205, 207,
    209-212, 214, 217, 231, 239, 240, 248
Stiff   38
Summer marks   49
Sunrise III   183
Sverre Haver   52
Swan Hunter   36, 42
Swiss Cheese Model   1-3, 12, 14, 67, 108, 118, 214, 250

T

T2 tanker   42, 64, 75, 188, 215
Taconite pellets   23
Tank cleaning   114
Tank-top   38, 39, 195
Teesside   36, 37, 42, 84, 94, 100
Tender   16, 133, 175, 238, 239
Tasca   150, 152, 156
Tetra-ethyl lead   49, 51
Texas City Oil Refinery   97-99
The Long Blue Line   162, 163
The Theory and Practice of Seamanship   49
Three Mile Island   233
Titanic   116
TOTE   148, 165, 166, 168-170, 174, 175
Townsend Car Ferries Limited   80, 81, 89, 94
Typhoon Orchid   36, 43
Typhoon Vernon   44

U

UK Department of Transport   55
UNCLOS   240

United Nations   182, 198, 205, 227, 229, 240, 244
United States Coastguard   13
Universal Bulk Carrier   67
University of Glasgow   58
Until the Sea Shall Free Them   13, 65, 71, 159, 161
US Chemical and Investigation Board   98
US Merchant Marine   78, 160

V

VDR   197, 198
Viking Sally   105
Viking Sky   240, 241
Vladimir Lenin   129
VLCC   114, 115, 121, 122, 183-186, 211, 212, 217
VLOC   184, 186, 202, 204, 205, 211, 217
Voyage Data Recorder   176, 177, 182, 198, 199, 209, 231, 239

W

Waratah   48, 49
Warsash Maritime school   8
Watertight doors   81, 85, 86, 91, 92
Welland Canal   17
World Expo   16

Y

Yellow ribbon   136, 137, 140
Yonhap   177
Yoo Byung-eun   139

Z

Zeebrugge   13, 80, 85, 86, 103, 113, 216, 237

Made in the USA
Middletown, DE
14 June 2019